**Other books by Cathy Covell**

*A Patient's Guide to Understanding
Myofascial Release*

*A Therapist's Guide to Understanding
Myofascial Release*

# Feeling Your Way Through

## Cathy Covell

**BALBOA.**
PRESS

A DIVISION OF HAY HOUSE

Balboa Press books may be ordered through booksellers or by contacting:

Balboa Press
A Division of Hay House
1663 Liberty Drive
Bloomington, IN 47403
www.balboapress.com
1 (877) 407-4847

Because of the dynamic nature of the Internet, any web addresses or links contained in this book may have changed since publication and may no longer be valid. The views expressed in this work are solely those of the author and do not necessarily reflect the views of the publisher, and the publisher hereby disclaims any responsibility for them.

The author of this book does not dispense medical advice or prescribe the use of any technique as a form of treatment for physical, emotional, or medical problems without the advice of a physician, either directly or indirectly. The intent of the author is only to offer information of a general nature to help you in your quest for emotional and spiritual well-being. In the event you use any of the information in this book for yourself, which is your constitutional right, the author and the publisher assume no responsibility for your actions.

Any people depicted in stock imagery provided by Thinkstock are models, and such images are being used for illustrative purposes only.
Certain stock imagery © Thinkstock.

Printed in the United States of America.

ISBN: 978-1-4525-8954-1 (sc)
ISBN: 978-1-4525-8956-5 (hc)
ISBN: 978-1-4525-8955-8 (e)

Library of Congress Control Number: 2014900170

Balboa Press rev. date: 1/22/2014

# Contents

# Special Thanks

There are so many who have helped me in one way or another along my journey and with the creation of this book. There is no way I can list them all. So, to all of you, I want to say thank you from the bottom of my heart.

To the pioneers who have paved the way through their books and seminars, I want to say thank you again. There are some who I want to thank specifically: John F. Barnes for introducing me to Myofascial Release. I thought I was just going to find a tool to help reduce physical pain; instead, I discovered a whole new way to look at life. Pema Chödrön, Caroline Myss, Dr. Wayne Dyer, Don Miguel Ruiz, Paulo Coelho, Deepak Chopra: your books and seminars were vital in my journey and in the journey of so many others. Thank you for being willing to share your truths with others.

Also, to some of my friends who have truly been angels in my life and who helped support me in the process of writing this book, thank you for your love and your support. Again, there are so many for whom I am grateful. I would like to mention a few: Angie Balsmeyer, Heather Christlieb, Amanda Davis, Valerie McGraw, Leanne Lafuze, Shelly Shulz-Borris, Tonya Windsor.

And of course thanks to Joe Miller for editing the original draft of this book for structure, content, and clarity, and for proofreading the final draft for this printing. I am sure it turned out to be more of a project than you thought it would be and I really appreciate your suggestions (content and wording choices here are mine alone) and your help! Thanks to Julie Fox for reading the final version and finding places that needed clarity. And of course thanks to the legendary office goddess Brianne Radtke: without you, I wouldn't have a life! ☺

*Cathy Covell*

# *Feeling Your Way Through*

**Author's Note**

When did feeling, or, I should say, feeling uncomfortable sensations, become the enemy? It seems it has become a goal in life to avoid feeling anything even slightly uncomfortable, especially emotions. When did the switch occur from feeling to thinking? Why have we been taught to disregard one of the most important guidance systems we have?

Conventional medicine and the traditional mindset in general have long tried to negate feeling. It has become more and more apparent that many holistic and spiritual teachings are doing the same thing. Traditional healthcare tries to numb us with medicine, and, unfortunately, so do some kinds of holistic approaches. Similarly, some spiritual practices try to numb us with too much focus on detachment, on thinking, or on not feeling. There seem to be several beliefs common to all of these: we should feel good all the time; if we are experiencing physical pain, negative feelings, or any kind of chaos in our life, we are doing something wrong; if we just took this particular pill, or changed our thoughts, we could be happy all the time.

I have found a different truth: to become actually and fully present, centered, enlightened—or whatever term you want to call it—you need to be able to feel your way through. We need to learn how to tune in to our inner guidance system and use the guidance we receive for true growth and healing. This guidance comes in the form of sensations, both pleasant and unpleasant; both are important. Rather than judging sensations as good or bad, we need to learn how to trust them for what they are: guidance. It's not just traditional science that needs to hear this message; many practices termed holistic either focus on avoiding sensations or simply categorize them as creations of the mind. This mindset robs us of a very important guidance system, a tool meant to help increase our awareness and presence, an essential part of our makeup that can lead to uncovering our true self.

In this book, I attempt to provide some insights that can help guide you along your healing path. I hope to be able to help you tap into your inner guidance system, your feelings. This book also provides some basic information about some kinds of body work that can help you access and release the physical and emotional restrictions that may be preventing your growth.

Each person's journey toward enlightenment and spiritual growth is unique. I am attempting to help you further your knowledge of the importance of the body's and spirit's wisdom and also to provide you with more tools to use along your journey. This information comes from my own journey and the insights I have had along the way. My journey is my own process of feeling through my physical and emotional traumas; of uncovering my limiting beliefs, thoughts, and judgments; and of coming along my own healing path. As I have uncovered truths for myself, I have realized they are universal truths. In life, these truths are presented in many different ways, through many different sources. This book is an accumulation of things that have helped me along my path and that have also come together as I have helped others. As with any book, seminar, or lecture, take what works for you and disregard what doesn't. My hope in writing this book is to help others as I have been helped myself. Enjoy your journey.

*Cathy Covell*

# Introduction: Enlightenment

How do I become enlightened? How do I find peace or balance in my life? How do I heal? What is my life's purpose? How do I regain my function? How can I become happy? These are just a few of the questions you might have asked yourself at some time. The search for answers to these questions drives us to read books, take seminars, and seek healers and spiritual counselors, among many other approaches.

If you are reading this book, you have probably asked one or more of these questions yourself. For each question, is there a single answer right for each person who asks? No. The answer to each question is unique for you and for every other person who asks. The path that leads to uncovering your answers is also different from the one anyone else takes. Somewhere along the way, every person discovers that the answers he or she has been seeking outside can only be found by turning within.

By uncovering your own truths and beliefs, and discarding those that aren't yours, you uncover the wisdom contained within you. How do you learn to tap into your inner guide and wisdom? For one thing, you truly need to learn how to listen to and connect with the knowledge and the consciousness that are part of your body's essence.

Countless books and seminars address enlightenment, healing trauma, breaking free of negative thinking, and other aspects of personal growth. Some talk about the need for positive thinking or try to teach you to use positive statements designed to help you change your life; some go so far as to say you can manifest anything into your life just by thinking positively enough. Others teach you how to become aware of your beliefs and, in turn, of the effects your beliefs have on your life. Still others focus on meditation, breathing exercises, and other practices as means for reaching a state of peace or enlightenment. These books and seminars may have invaluable insights into increasing your awareness and progressing along your quest for self-fulfillment, healing, and spiritual development. Many have helped people make significant shifts in their lives and improvements in their awareness.

These resources have a common focus on bringing awareness to your thoughts; many also talk about connecting to your inner guide or your intuition to help guide you along your journey. They teach that it is the mind, the ego, or whatever the term used, that creates all the problems with triggers we battle, that the mind is the cause of all our suffering. They talk about how the constant chatter in our mind is hindering our growth or our attainment of peace and so also our healing. These books and seminars provide some excellent ways to help bring our awareness to our thoughts and to see how we are creating our own misery.

I have found the books and seminars that focus on thought are missing an essential element in the search for enlightenment, peace, and healing: the guidance and wisdom inherent in the body. Every cell in the body has consciousness, has the ability to communicate with the entire body, and can store memories. Our focus needs to include more than just the mind if we want to completely release trauma, negative beliefs, or negative patterns; we must feel the connection to these things in our body if we are to move into true healing. Feeling allows us to get to the root of our struggles and helps bring about change at the cellular level. Feeling through the trauma, the negative beliefs, the negative patterns, is essential if we want truly to live in the present, instead of always fighting triggers from our past.

To live fully and completely in the present, we need to be aware of our thoughts and also to become aware of the guidance from our body. There may be places in our body that are storing beliefs or emotions from the past. We need to know where such old beliefs or emotions are located *in our body* and how to release them *from our body* so we can truly be free. People often have problems implementing the ideas they find in books that focus only on the aspect of healing involving the thoughts or the mind; when they try to bring these ideas to bear on their lives, they still have the same triggers taking control again. No matter how hard they try, they still get triggered. They may be more aware of being triggered; they may be able to think logically about, and dissociate from, reacting to the triggers; but they are still being triggered. This is because the triggers and the triggering do not happen in the mind alone. Tissue memory in the body can be triggered, causing the automatic response that comes from the body and not from the mind. This book will help you learn how to truly communicate with the body, find tissue memory triggers in the body, and release those triggers from the body. There is a language of the body; once you learn how to free this language, you can fully connect your mind, body, and spirit.

The missing link in healing involves feeling—feeling in your body for the answers you have sought outside of yourself. You add this missing link by unleashing your inner wisdom, by making the mind-body-spirit connection; doing this will be a catalyst to help you achieve the balance and peace you seek. You can finally release yourself from the control of your triggers by making the mind-body-spirit connection and helping your body open up tissue that contains cellular or tissue memory. Until then, you're not acting; you're reacting. Your mind cannot prevent the tissue memory or the body's reactions to that memory, no matter how hard it tries. Combining mind-body-spirit awareness with bodywork that releases physical restrictions (bodywork such as JFB-MFR) can help resolve core issues so you don't have to keep fighting these triggers; you can actually release them and progress to complete healing.

As I said earlier, each person's journey is unique. One thing common to all paths is that no one grows in his or her comfort zone. Growth takes going into your fears and may take going into chaos as well. To make real change in anything you are doing, you have to go into the uncomfortable feelings and sensations. This is why trying to achieve a state in which there is no chaos is actually counterproductive to growth. Given the ever-changing, dynamic nature of life (which could be called chaos), going into the uncomfortable feelings is what leads to growth.

It often takes something uncomfortable to cause us to take action and change. Sometimes this discomfort comes as emotional distress, when you feel depressed, sad, or angry. Sometimes it takes physical distress before you will be ready to grow into the next layer. Sometimes it takes an injury, a trauma, before you will take the time to stop and look at what you are supposed to heal. When you stop trying to avoid these uncomfortable feelings, and turn into them instead, you may find out they were actually a gift in disguise. This is why people often have periods of suffering right before they have a spiritual growth. If you read about the lives of spiritual masters, you find many went through what the poet Saint John of the Cross described as "the dark night of the soul;" they went through a time, or many times, when they felt lost, when they struggled and then came to peace with their core fears and beliefs. To become a master, to become enlightened, this struggle must occur.

You do not need to have a particular belief, religious or otherwise, to benefit from uncovering your inner wisdom. All the teachings come from the same truths, from universal truths. Some of the terms I use in this book may be different from ones you use to mean the same thing; the richness is the same regardless of the terms each of us may use. For instance, I write about inner wisdom and inner guidance; in the Bible these are called the Holy Spirit. Other religions or belief systems use other terms. As you read this book, change my words to ones that feel right for you. I write about various spiritual masters and many others in the realm of spiritual practice. Spiritual masters found their own unique path; they started on one path and were guided along the way to many other paths. The key to growth is having the wisdom to know when to change paths or even to create your own path. Anytime you get in a mindset that there is only one way, you close yourself off from paths you may actually need to take to reach your next level of growth.

In this book, I offer tools, perceptions, and options to try out as you make your way along your path. This book can work along with any thought pattern or religious belief you may hold. Take only what works for you, what seems right for your path, and be willing to be open to new ideas and thoughts. As you read this book, if you feel I am speaking directly to you or you really connect with what I'm saying, you are ready for what this book has to say to you. If you find yourself trying to force your way through this book, then the message isn't for you at this time. This goes for any other book you try to read. At any moment, there is an author or a speaker with whom you will be able to connect and understand fully; that person is the one meant to help you along the way in the next step of your journey.

This is how you find your own path. You open yourself up to the knowledge around you by listening to lectures, reading books, joining discussion groups, going to seminars. As you connect with what is being shared, you will find your truths being revealed within you. You will find some of the things people say connect and resonate with you fully and others do not.

I have divided this book into the following sections, each discussing a broad topic.

**Section 1** is on losing ourselves, how we have lost ourselves throughout life.

**Section 2** discusses reconnecting to the body's wisdom.

**Section 3** talks about applying universal principles to the physical body so as to help release physical restrictions from the body. Applying these principles as discussed will enable you to become aware of and to release not only the physical restrictions in the body, but also the fears and beliefs that may be trapped in your subconscious and preventing your growth. This section also discusses an excellent tool for releasing, a form of bodywork called John F. Barnes' Myofascial Release (JFB-MFR).

**Section 4** is on awareness and choice. Once you become aware, you have to make the active choice to heal. Healing isn't a passive event. It's an active sport.

**Section 5** is about returning to your true self. This means uncovering your shadows, and your false beliefs and thoughts, all of which can keep you from growing and healing.

**Section 6** is about putting it all together and includes some final tips for healing and growth. I hope I have put these pieces together in a way that shows how everything fits together.

I've mentioned healing a number of times and I want to clarify what I mean. What does it mean to heal or to be healed? Many people think healing means one thing and one thing only: you are completely cured. By this definition, you're healed when you're completely, one-hundred percent functional, when something is completely gone from your body. This idea of healing implies you will never again be triggered or have chaos in your life. Complete healing does occur and has occurred (though without the part about never again being triggered or experiencing chaos); I have seen it myself and it often defies reason. However, you can really set yourself up for disappointment by thinking of healing as an absolute state, as some kind of fixed end point.

I think a better idea of healing is implied in the question Caroline Myss suggests we ask ourselves: "What is my highest potential at this time?" I really like the focus in this question because it's about living up to your highest potential at all times, rather than about being perfect or about feeling good. Healing is active and does not reach some set point. Healing, like life itself, includes chaos and always has cycles. There will always be times of change, which means you will be growing and expanding for the rest of your life.

This book can help you clear your physical and emotional restrictions and open yourself up to your highest potential. Your highest potential may be a complete healing. Your highest potential may be that you do not heal completely in the physical sense and that you see your experience as a gift you can use to help others to heal and grow. To reach your highest potential, you may have to go through loss and trials to uncover strength you have yet to recognize.

Before you continue reading this book, make a list of aspects of your life in which you would like guidance, improvement, or change. Write down specific goals, desires, and ideas. If you need help with this, read

Chapter 20, *The Importance of Goals*. Having some clear intention is a really great way to open yourself to guidance. Be open to the possibility of healing and growing to your fullest potential. Then let go of the limits and enjoy this book and your journey!

## Section 1

*How Do We*

*Lose Ourselves?*

## Chapter 1

### The Restrictions We Have at Birth

If you have had the opportunity to hold a newborn and look deeply into that child's eyes, you have had the chance to see and feel the deep connection that young spirit has with the divine, or what I call God. If you open up your heart and connect fully with the eyes of a newborn, you can feel that connection. If you've had the opportunity to hold many children, you know it's easier to feel this connection with some children than with others. Some kids seem to have a lightness or an easiness about them, a strong sense of self, while others seem to be born with a heaviness of spirit and body and an emotional instability.

It appears we are actually born with some degree of restriction in our physical and emotional bodies. How could this be? Our light source, or soul, enters our physical form before birth. Every one of us has an essence and that essence is placed inside our physical form, our body, a body made up of millions of cells. Where do the cells come from? These cells did not spontaneously generate; they came from our parents. Our mother's and our father's cells came from their parents, and so on all the way back through our family tree. What does this have to do with being born with particular restrictions or characteristics?

Cells can have cellular or tissue memory. Recent research reveals cells contain consciousness and tissue memory. This tissue memory or consciousness can pass down through the generations in the cells that make up our body. These cells can carry the beliefs, traumas (both physical and emotional), mannerisms, likes and dislikes, and other traits of our ancestors. This ancestral tissue memory can be passed along to us in the form of the physical body with which we are born; it can also influence the degree of restriction or of heaviness with which we are born.

Another factor affecting the degree of restriction with which we are born is the physical and emotional trauma occurring in the birth process. Birth is a life or death struggle for both the baby and the mother, and each birth is unique. The birth process can cause a wide variety of physical traumas; the natural forces and the human interventions in birth can dislocate a shoulder or a hip, or torsion the pelvis or the cranium. Added to this, many babies are instantly poked and prodded and suctioned... a really nice welcome to the world! The traditional western birthing process often inflicts a lot of unnecessary trauma on a newborn.

So, we see a child's cellular makeup and birth process combine to influence how much ease of spirit the child has at birth. I'll use the following example to expand on what I'm saying. Think of our essence as a light bulb and our physical body as a globe containing the light bulb. If the globe is filmy or dirty, the light from the bulb is dim. If you compare two lights, each with a bulb of the same wattage but one with a clean globe and the other with a filmy globe, you find the brightness of the light depends on the cleanliness of the globe. The physical and emotional traumas residing in our physical form from our cellular memory and our birth are like the film on the globe. The more buildup of trauma, the duller the light, or the more heaviness, in a person. The soul, or essence, we have inside of our physical form is brilliant, vibrant, beautiful. Sometimes the soul's light is limited by the nature of our physical form. If our tissue has restrictions, it is tight and dense (and the cells can be tight and dense too), and this essence doesn't shine through brightly, just as the film on the globe keeps the light from the bulb from shining brightly.

This is apparent in the differences among children. Some children just have a lightness about them from birth. They're open. They laugh easily. They are joyful and just seem to bring out joy in others. They sleep easily and do not mind being alone. At the other end of this spectrum are the children who are born fearful, are withdrawn, have a hard time sleeping, are usually colicky, and do not seem at ease with themselves. They are not at ease in this physical form. Of course, there is the entire range between these two extremes.

This is a brief description of some of the restrictions and limitations that we can have at birth. In the next chapter, I discuss other layers of film that can be put on the globe during our upbringing. The way we are raised can bring out our brightness or it can add to the restrictions that limit our brilliance.

Chapter 2

*Our Programming*

During our upbringing, we can lose our connection to our intuition or to our true selves. The upbringing process is sometimes called our programming process; author Don Miguel Ruiz calls it the domestication process. This is the process by which the many influences in our lives—among others, our family, our community, our state, our country—shape how we develop our beliefs, values, and judgments. One of our biggest influences tends to be our family. Passing down family traditions, beliefs, ideals, thoughts, and judgments instills generation after generation with ideas of what is right or wrong, of how we should and shouldn't act, of what to believe or feel in different situations.

In the early years of his life, a child is powerfully influenced by either the encouragement to keep the connection to god and the true self, or the programming to ignore this connection so as to conform to the beliefs of his family or community. For example, a child raised in a family full of fears—or in one that does not encourage the child to tap into his own wisdom—can become full of fear himself and, in turn, lose the connection to his truth. The fear will cause the child to be reactive instead of being able to respond from his truth. Such a child (and others in similar situations) is taught how to judge, to behave, to modify his own thoughts and feelings, so he pleases those around him. In a given situation, instead of responding in a way that is truthful, he will hesitate and come up with an answer he believes will be the correct in this particular situation. He will try to speak, behave, and think in a way that will bring positive reinforcement from those around him.

This is part of what many call programming or the domestication process. This programming becomes so automatic that it rules our subconscious. Most people do not live; they react as they have been programmed to do. Consider driving as an example of programming. When we are first learning to drive, we really have to concentrate. We think about every part of the process—timing when to put on turn signals, remembering to check the mirrors, keeping an eye on how fast we are going, concentrating on which route we will be taking. Over time, these and all the other behaviors of driving become second nature. Pretty soon, when we pull out on the street, we are usually thinking about other things and are on what we call autopilot. We know which side of the road to go on, what to do at a stop sign and at a stop light, when to turn on the signals and lights, etc. We aren't really thinking and concentrating fully each moment we are driving, unless perhaps we are in a new area and have to pay attention to what is unfamiliar.

The same sort of programming is at work when we look around a room; we often go on autopilot if there's nothing unusual or unfamiliar about the room or its contents. We tend to dismiss whatever looks familiar, and knowing the name of something has a lot to do with its looking familiar. We were taught the names of things, what color is and the names of colors, the language itself. Everything is taught to us—what is red and what is blue; what is a table, a light, a salt or pepper shaker. As we are taught the name of something, we are also taught its use, its proper location, whether and when it's appropriate. We are often taught with the reward/punishment method. If you provide the correct answer or do the correct thing, you are rewarded with food or praise, or sometimes even with money. If you give an incorrect answer or do the wrong thing, you are scolded or humiliated, or you have things taken away from you; you might even be punished physically. We learn quickly to provide the right answer according to the information we have been given. We come to understand that we need to learn and memorize the correct answer not only to fit in, but also to be rewarded or praised. So we learn that what's important is thinking and memorizing, rather than feeling our truth.

We are taught to ignore our intuition and body senses, and instead to rely on our mind and on whatever we have been told is right or wrong in a given situation. For example, when a child doesn't want to hug a relative, he is often scolded and told, "That's Uncle Jim and he gave you a present, so you need to hug him!" This child's intuition may be saying, "I don't trust that adult." But he is trained to ignore his protective intuition and instead is taught that when an adult—especially a relative—gives him something, that means he owes the adult something in return. In this situation the child is told he owes a hug. The child is being taught that he shouldn't listen to what his intuition is telling him about this person, that it is more important to do what has been taught as "right" than to listen to what is truth to him. This mixed signal—to ignore what your body, your spirit, or your intuition is telling you, and to do instead what your mind tells you is right—is the unintended and tragic cause that often leads children into being victims of molestation or other forms of abuse. This is particularly true when you're taught that if someone gives you something, or is nice to you, then you owe them something in return, even if it doesn't feel right to you.

Children are often (and generally unintentionally) taught to ignore danger signals coming from the true self and to do instead the things they have been programmed to believe are right. Some children are taught that their wants, feelings, and thoughts aren't important. They learn they need to listen to and respect adults, and that adults—especially those in authority positions—know better than children. These teachings can lead a child into confusion when an adult in a trusted position—a priest, a school teacher, a relative—wants to do inappropriate things with and to the child. This can severely damage a child's sense of trust, especially with trusting himself. The child is taught not to listen to his true self and, instead, to trust fully that adults will protect him, and then he gets hurt. He may sense that he shouldn't trust a particular adult, but he is taught to give his power to the adult rather than to trust his own judgment, and he ends up hurt. After that, he often loses faith in the rules he was taught and told to believe, and also loses trust in himself.

Carolyn Myss raised this subject at a seminar I attended on her book *Defy Gravity*. She stated that abuse or trauma at an early age can "throw off the compass" of a child. A child's compass of who he is supposed to trust can be thrown off completely when the child is abused by someone in his tribe, community, or family, and the abuser is someone the child is supposed to recognize as a protector or as trustworthy. This kind of experience damages the child's trust in himself, and in others, because what he was taught to believe—that these adults in his family or community protect him—ends up being a lie; the people he was taught to listen to, even when he knew in truth he shouldn't trust them, ended up harming him. This can make it hard for the child to connect with his own inner guidance to get his own sense of what is right and what is wrong.

I feel that establishing boundaries, while also teaching children to listen to their own truth, must be one of a parent's hardest jobs. It is very difficult to give a child a set of boundaries and also teach him to trust his own intuition and his own sense of what feels appropriate. How do you raise empowered children? How do you encourage them to think and feel for themselves, while also providing some boundaries within which they can live and function effectively in society? It can be done, but it generally requires parents and other adults in the community to break free of the programming they themselves were taught as children. Usually, we tend to do as parents what our own parents did with us when we were children, and that tendency is passed down through the generations. The tendency to do with our children as our parents used to do with us is itself part of the domestication process and also part of the reason the domestication process continues through the generations.

## Chapter 3

### *Beliefs and Judgments*

Every child is instilled with different beliefs and judgments throughout her life. These beliefs, judgments, and rules vary depending on the ideals of her family, community, and country. Some of the beliefs are based on her family's religion, ethnicity, and family dynamics. Others are influenced by the community, state, and country in which she is raised. The ideas of "right" and "wrong," the rules and laws, the work standards, and so on, vary across families, communities, regions, and so forth. If you have traveled outside of your own community or country, you have seen a huge variety in versions of "normal," "right," "wrong," "appropriate," and "inappropriate," depending on the beliefs of the people in the places you have visited. If you ask people in these various places to tell you their beliefs about which way is "right," they will usually say their way is "right." In the extreme, this is what leads to wars—proving that "I am right." We are usually taught we need to defend what we think or believe is right and to prove other ways of thinking or believing are wrong.

Let's look at some examples of different versions of normal. Consider the matter of punctuality. Some families are always fifteen minutes early to functions; other families are always running late. In either case, what they do defines what is normal to them. This seems like an insignificant thing, but it is a clear and simple example of how beliefs can get passed down. Other, less neutral, beliefs can also be passed down, beliefs about which race is dominant, which religion is the right religion, how men or women should wear their hair, what clothes are appropriate or inappropriate, what constitutes legitimate marriage, who should be allowed to marry and when. In the United States, it seems to be a normal belief that it's okay for a man to marry a younger woman; however, a woman is often criticized for marrying a younger man. While norms concerning interracial, interfaith, and intercultural marriages have changed significantly in the past century, people are still ostracized and even murdered for these kinds of marriages in some countries. These are just a few examples of how widely the definition of "normal" can vary.

Other things, such as preferences or tastes in food, can seem minor, but they have an impact on us just the same. For instance, my family was pretty much "meat and potatoes," and the only spices I knew growing up were salt and pepper. When I started traveling and went to Louisiana, I had quite a shock when I got a taste of what another part of the world considered spices! Sometimes, the process of coming to understand that you don't know what is out there is a wonderful experience; learning about a whole new world of spices was a wonderful experience. But what traveling really helped me start to learn is that everyone's version of "normal" is different, from the food we eat and the clothes we wear, to the words we use and our beliefs about etiquette and rules.

My years of traveling as a contract therapist really helped me to understand the regional differences in the United States. When I traveled in Europe, I was exposed to an even greater diversity in cultures and beliefs. We spend most of our life trying to figure out how to follow the rules of life, and we find out the rules change everywhere we go! Everybody's version of "normal" and "right" can be different wherever you go. This can be either very scary or very freeing. It can be scary in that we were taught that if we don't do what is "right," we will be punished. Without knowing the basic rules to follow in a given situation, we could do the "wrong" thing, which could lead to punishment. However, looked at another way, this can be such freedom! We don't have to follow the rules set by others; we can start to do what is right for us. Choosing to do what is truly right for your soul is very different from being like a two year old who says, "I am going to do it because I want to!" It's freeing to learn on your own what is right for your heart and soul, instead of doing what you've been told to do even if it doesn't feel good to your heart and soul. You can be opened up to a world you didn't even know exists, if you are willing to view an unfamiliar situation as exactly that: a situation you didn't know could exist. But, if you are raised to believe that different is scary and wrong, then discovering there is so much variety in the world can be very threatening and scary. This is what can lead to violence and war.

If you were taught to believe that what is different is wrong, that you should fear people and cultures that are different from you, that the way you were raised or taught is the only way and the right way, your beliefs can become an anchor that tethers you to fear. Being in this kind of fear can hinder your growth. You may have been instilled through your upbringing with the thought that if you don't do what is deemed "right," you will be punished or ostracized. You may have been taught that you will spend eternity in punishment or hell if you don't follow the rules.

Some people are raised being punished severely for asking questions or questioning authority. You may have been taught to just "do what you are told." Many of us have heard "because I said so" when we asked "why" one too many times; we also might have responded in the same way to that same question. We were taught not to be curious, but rather to learn the set of rules to follow so that we will be rewarded and not punished. The idea of going within yourself and feeling for your true answers is not something typically cultivated in our learning process. Because of this, you may have lost some or all of the ability to go into yourself, to question and feel for yourself. You may have been taught instead to surrender your power to higher authorities or to rules established, in some cases, centuries ago.

By the time we reach adulthood, most of us have been taught and have embraced a solid system of beliefs, even if these beliefs run our lives and do not truly match how we feel. We pretty much run on autopilot. Such beliefs are about things like how we should wear our hair, what religion we should be, what is appropriate to say or do. These beliefs often have as little feeling or emotion around them as there is around knowing that red means stop and green means go on a traffic light. We don't usually put much thought into how we really feel about the things we believe. Our beliefs just become "the way it is;" but this can lead to us becoming numb, and, pretty soon, instead of living life, we're just surviving it. We can fall into a rut or a routine, and, day in and day out, we just go through the motions of life following the beliefs and patterns that were set up for us. We follow patterns like, "By this age I should marry; then I should have kids," or, "I should work go to work so I can obtain these things that I am supposed to buy, and that will make me happy." We are being run by such beliefs, not living each day. We have lost our connection to our spirit; we have lost our reverence for our own life and the lives of others. We are spiritually shut down.

If you feel or believe you don't tend to be judgmental or don't have judgments going through your mind all the time, just try this exercise. The next time you're walking or driving, take twenty minutes and just be aware of every person, house, and car you see; just notice how many judgments pop into your head. As you see people, notice how many judgments come up based on how they look, walk, dress, wear their hair. Notice how your judgments lead to you to be attracted to some people and repelled from others. Now consider each house you see. Is it the right color, the wrong color, messy? Does it need repairs? The car—too fancy, too old, too loud? Just take notice of how much your mind is going. You will likely notice you are judging and categorizing all the time. We are taught to do this in our families and at school, and we learn it quite well. As you become aware of these judgments, you can decide which among them are ones you truly believe and which are ones you learned but aren't really true to you. This is how you can start uncovering your true self instead of being controlled by judgments and beliefs that are not your own.

## Chapter 4

*Masks and Insanity*

At some point in life, we will realize that no matter how hard we try to follow the rules, we will never be "good enough" when we measure ourselves by others' standards. We come to understand that just when we think we have figured out the rules, the rules will change. We find that no matter how hard we try to follow all the rules, we can't be what everyone else wants us to be. This is when we start to create the different masks we present to others, a behavior I call everyone's own form of insanity.

As we grow up, we learn we can act a certain way—wear one mask—at our home, but need to act differently (wear a different mask) at our grandparents' home. Gradually, we learn we need to be a different person, or wear another mask, when we go to church, and need yet other masks when we are at a store, in public, at school. We learn we must juggle these masks, trying to determine which one we need to wear, or which person we need to be, depending on our current situation and on the people around us. We act differently around our family than we do around our friends, with strangers, or at social gatherings. Juggling all these masks, changing who we are depending on the situation, can become confusing and exhausting. This is when we can lose track of our true self.

In counseling, people with multiple personality disorders are labeled schizophrenic. It seems to me everyone has a multiple personality disorder; some of us get completely consumed by the multiple personalities and some of us learn to manage them. I am not saying schizophrenia is not a serious disorder; it is serious and needs to be managed by professionals. However, I am saying that if we define multiple personality disorder as having different voices in our heads, then all of us can claim to struggle with this issue. These different voices can come from the multiple masks we have learned to create. We can easily fall into identifying with our masks, and, in so doing, lose connection with our true self. This is the result of being taught that who we are truly, that our true self, isn't appropriate or should be changed.

As it turns out, no matter how hard we try to wear the "right" mask for each situation, we still end up doing things "wrong." Sooner or later, we say or do something, or behave in some way, which gets us into trouble; or we are ridiculed, which can cause us emotional pain. Whether in trouble or ridiculed when we fail to wear the "right" mask, we can find ourselves believing something is wrong with us. It can be very traumatic when we are told, or we take on the message, that who we are isn't good enough.

It's so easy to wear the "wrong" mask. For example, when we're little, we might do something at home that our family thinks is funny, so we keep doing it because it causes our family to laugh and brings us positive reinforcement. Then we go out in public and we do the same thing, and it's not funny; instead, it's deemed inappropriate and we are punished because of it. We can't understand what happened. One minute the way we act is funny and brings us positive attention, and the next minute it's not funny and causes us to be punished. We are confused and learn that the rules do not follow a logical system. This can seem like a simple and insignificant incident, but as these incidents build up over time, they can create a very significant pattern.

We might also have what seem to be more significant incidents, ones in which wearing no mask at all ends up being "wrong." For example, you might make a mistake during a sporting event and your father belittles you in front of everyone or even says that he is embarrassed to have you as a son. You might speak a truth in front of a group of peers and they make fun of you or call you stupid. You might really open up when talking about a thought or idea of yours, one that is very dear to your heart, and you get a response like, "That will never happen" or "What are you thinking?" or "That's ridiculous."

In these moments, when we find we're in trouble or ridiculed for wearing the wrong mask or no mask, we can start to lose our true self and learn that we need to put on the false masks. Even though it may not be apparent, these incidents leave emotional wounds that can cause damage and start us questioning or disliking our true self. We have been taught that good things happen when we do things right and bad things happen when we do something wrong. So, when we are speaking or acting from our truth and we get punished or ridiculed, we are likely to hurt. Within the context of punishment and reward, we learn that if we hurt, we must have done something wrong and that means there must be something wrong with us.

When you end up feeling like there is something wrong with you in situations like these, you can have the very traumatic experience of feeling like a part of you is dying. It can feel like you are losing any sense of foundation in your life. You can't trust your true self to guide you because doing so sometimes leads to punishment. You can't trust the rules established by your family, friends, and society because those rules are always changing. So, who can you trust? What can you believe?

When we are young, we depend on our family for support and protection. We don't really have the option of being true to ourselves no matter what; doing so would lead to punishment and perhaps even to being ostracized from the family. As times goes on, it may seem there is no option other than trying to conform to the ever-changing rules, putting on different masks, and choosing to believe that learning how to do things "right" means we won't be punished or ridiculed, even though we know all of this is a lie. It feels safer to us to believe this lie. It feels safer to take on the belief that if we are punished, hurt, or ridiculed, it is because we must have done something "wrong," rather than to admit to ourselves the truth that no matter how hard we try, we will have pain and hurt come into our lives. We sell our truth for the safety of belonging to a group, for what we call love, for some sense of security. This is true insanity. Trying to make yourself believe a lie divides your soul against itself. Nevertheless, we often try to live with this lie and the divided soul that comes with it, setting aside our need to be true to our spirit. We do this believing we can avoid being punished by or cast out from our family or community, or even being killed, for living our truth.

As we become adults, we have choices that give us opportunities to break free of the lies and start living our truth. Throughout our lives, we are put in situations that will lead us to ask ourselves, "Are you going to start being true to yourself, or are you going to keep selling out your soul?" We have this choice to make with our relationships, our careers, our health, and even our time. Think of how many times you have heard someone say, "I don't love my husband, but I don't think I can make it on my own." Or, "I hate my job, but I won't be able to sustain my current lifestyle by following my passion." Both of these are examples of selling yourself for financial security. Consider the people who end a relationship because of the racial or social prejudices of their friends, family, or society. This is selling out your soul for the approval of others. This list of situations in which you might choose to sell out your soul can go on and on, and fear is at the root of every situation in the list: you could be punished; you could be harassed; you could be disowned by your family; in some countries you could be killed for loving someone of the "wrong" race, sex, or social status. As an adult, you have and can make the choice not to sell out your soul for security, for approval, or for any other reason. For example, as an adult, you have the legal right to leave your family; you can choose to try to support yourself. Still, many of us still let these fears control us.

Growing, healing, uncovering our true selves, sounds like a wonderfully beautiful adventure, and the end result is beautiful. But the path to it is full of all the fears, demons, and hurts that caused you to hide yourself behind masks in the first place. To break free and release the beauty from the inside, you must first uncover and face the fears and hurts that keep you trapped. In the process of growing and healing to reach the beauty underneath, you will need to feel your way through some very painful and scary things. This is why so many people stop the process. Somewhere along the way in your healing process, you might reach a point at which you feel like you are going insane. This tends to happen when you get to the core issues from those instances when you sold a piece of your soul. Those are the instances when you chose to try to force yourself to believe something you knew was a lie so you could fit in, be accepted, be secure, or be "loved." I put "love" in quotes in this instance because the type of love that requires you to be something other than your true self is conditional love, not real love.

Most of us have had experiences in which we either received a message, or interpreted events or comments as a message, that left our soul damaged and provoked us to put on a mask. These are messages saying you are inappropriate, you aren't good, right, or loveable. When events trigger the memory of such an experience, you have uncovered an instance when you decided it would be better to create a false image than to be true to yourself. Uncovering these experiences can be painful, but doing so is also a chance to liberate yourself. In times like these, you have the chance to feel fully whatever caused the split from your true self and to make a conscious decision to either continue to live a lie and damage your soul, or to live your truth and free your soul. This sounds like an easy choice, but it isn't always that simple. Remember, this could change everything in your life. You could lose your profession, your security, your relationship, or your family; you might even have your life threatened. Sometimes you can make the choice to be true to yourself immediately; in other instances, it may take some time to make this choice. You may have to uncover many layers and heal each of them before you can take that final step. This is when you need to remember to be gentle on yourself. Becoming aware that you are selling out a piece of your soul is a step in the direction of healing and growth. When you stop blaming others and take responsibility for yourself, you can start to heal and grow.

When you add to all this a lifetime of masks and hurts that are all interconnected, you really need to take a breath and remind yourself that healing this is a process. One hurt or mask connects with another, and that with yet another. Imagine unraveling a three dimensional web all tied in knots. All the strands are connected and as you start to untie one knot, it pulls on another. We have all had a lot of physical and emotional trauma in our lives. Untangling the physical trauma, the emotional trauma, the thoughts and beliefs that are all woven together, is something that can be done only with love, patience, and gentleness. Remind yourself you did the best you knew how to do at any moment. We all have built the masks. We all have sold and continue to sell pieces of ourselves. We all have self-doubt and self-judgment. We all have tried so hard to fit into the category of "normal" thinking in the belief that doing so would get us love and approval.

If you are reading this book, you have probably reached the point at which you no longer want to sell out your soul. You have decided it is time to break free and let out your true beauty. This chapter has suggested some of the reasons for our masks and insanity. I hope this information helps you decide it is time to start weaning from the masks and allowing your true, enlightened self to shine!

# Chapter 5

## *Physical and Emotional Traumas*

Another way one becomes bound down and disconnected from one's true self is through physical and emotional traumas. Can you separate the two? No, you can't. But in the physical and mental healthcare fields, that's exactly what's been tried, and it has led to a lot of needless suffering. I want to be very clear with the following point: every physical trauma has an emotional component, and every emotional trauma has a physical component. Trying to separate these two types of trauma is yet another way we can become split; it is also a reason so many people do not heal. Addressing emotions exclusively in a counseling setting, and physical symptoms in a healthcare setting (whether through physical or other body therapies, or through surgeries or other treatments), is hopeless; you are trying to separate a system that can't be separated.

If you injure yourself in a fall down the stairs, you have physical trauma that can lead to restrictions and pain, and you also have some sort of emotion associated with the trauma, likely some form of fear. You might feel anger if you fell down the stairs because you tripped on a towel someone left lying on one of the stairs. As you are falling, you might think, "I can't handle getting hurt" or "I can't afford to miss work." You may have been told not to go down the stairs; then, when you did it anyway and got hurt, you might judge your action as "wrong" and believe you deserved to be hurt as your punishment. All of these emotions, judgments, and beliefs can be intertwined with the physical trauma.

Take another example of a physical trauma that may also have an emotional element: a car accident. As you are driving, you see a car coming at you. You can't stop or get out of the way and, for an instant, you think, "I'm going to die." As the impact occurs, that thought and the fear that goes with it, along with the pain from the collision, can all get trapped within the tissue itself. The emotional component can become mixed with the bracing, guarding, and other kinds of physical reactions before impact, along with the actual cuts, bruises, and inflammation resulting from the impact.

Similarly, emotional trauma can have a physical component. Suppose you are attacked emotionally and feel as if you are being torn apart, although no one touches you physically. You will brace against this emotional attack just as if it were an actual physical attack. You will be guarding against the impact of the words as if they were actual physical blows. We often have this kind of experience when we lose a loved one. You can feel like your entire world is falling out from under you, that a part of you is dying. As you brace physically against the emotional assault, the physical and emotional restrictions become entwined. Your beliefs and judgments might add to this too. Was it wrong that your loved one died? Did you deserve to be assaulted emotionally?

How do these kinds of restrictions happen? *It's called life.* You are subjected to physical and emotional stresses on your body every day. If you were not taught how to release the restrictions that can result from these stresses, the restrictions build up over time. As they do, you become tighter and tighter. Your body starts to feel like it's in a straitjacket. Along with the traumas of daily life are profound traumas like child birth, infection, illness, car accidents, falls, death of loved ones… the list can go on. As we age, the restrictions caused by these traumas produce more and more pressure in the body and we start having mental, physical, or systemic breakdowns. This progression has been deemed the "normal" way of life, but it doesn't have to be so. It's considered normal because it's what the majority of people go through in their lives. But that is because we haven't been taught how to keep ourselves truly healthy. As you become aware of the physical restrictions in your body, of the emotions trapped within you, of the thoughts and beliefs creating your stress and keeping you out of balance, you can begin releasing them and returning to optimal health.

Section 2

# Reconnecting to the Body's Wisdom

## Chapter 6

# Everybody and Every Body is Unique

In the previous section, I described some ways you might have lost your connection to your true self throughout your life. In this section, I describe and explain some ways you can start to reconnect to your true self by learning how to listen to and understand the language of your body. By learning how to listen to the language of your body, you will uncover a tool that is extremely important in reconnecting to your true self. As you learn to listen and then feel through sensation—whether it's a physical or an emotional sensation—you will uncover the guidance of your inner wisdom, and that wisdom will help guide you along your path of growth and healing. When you feel through a sensation, you are connecting with the guidance of your inner wisdom. This concept is the source of this book's title. Tapping into and using the guidance and wisdom of your body and spirit, you are guided as you feel your way through sensations to connect to your true self. This will happen as you feel through the lies and judgments to your truth. To tap into this wisdom of your spirit, you need to learn to listen to the sensations you feel and to understand that those sensations are guidance that needs to be heard rather than covered up or avoided.

How do you start to listen to these messages? How do you start to uncover them? First, you need to understand what these sensations might mean and how to start using them as guidance. Later in this book, I describe how you can use your various sensations to help you distinguish your real truths from the messages coming from your false self. To help establish a basic understanding, I will make a division between physical and emotional sensations. As I have already discussed, this is an imaginary division in a realm that really can't be divided. Physical and emotional sensations are entirely connected. I divide them in the following discussion only to give some guidelines and to help describe some examples of different kinds of sensations and reasons you might feel them. But as you read about the reasons you might feel a given sensation, remember that each of us has a unique life and unique perceptions. So, as you uncover what you are feeling, be open to letting your own reasons evolve. Let go of any set path based on what others have discovered for themselves. No sensation can be defined or described in linear, black-and-white, logical, or $a + b = c$ terms. There may be some patterns, but nothing is set 100 percent.

We are dynamic beings and each of us has had our own, unique life experience. Our emotions and physical sensations can have many meanings at any given time. Whenever you categorize anything, you limit your growth. For instance, you limit yourself when you categorize anger as a "bad" or "negative" emotion and believe that, if you feel anger, then you need to meditate, because you shouldn't feel anger. Similarly, you limit yourself when you categorize seeing the color yellow as meaning you are happy, or having pain in your foot as meaning you are afraid to step forward.

Anytime you use a protocol, you are limiting your growth. When you use a protocol in this context, you are trying to force someone else's meaning of a sensation, a color, or a thought to fit you. Doing this will actually block you from authentic healing. This would be like trying to fit your foot in someone else's shoe; most of the times, another person's shoe won't fit you. This protocol mentality is also sometimes called using a "cookbook" or formula approach.

Remember that everybody and every body is different. Every body has had different physical and emotional traumas and stresses during its lifetime. Each person has unique perceptions of what those traumas and stresses mean. Each feeling, each sensation, each emotion, at any given time or in any given situation, may be completely different from one person to the next.

The following is an example of the uniqueness of experience. Suppose two people walk into a flower shop and see a red rose. One person smells the rose's scent and is taken back to a time when he gave the love of his life a rose; he feels love radiate through his body. The second person looks at that same rose, smells the same fragrance, and is reminded of a rose she just saw on her best friend's casket; she feels grief and sadness. Someone using the cookbook mentality might say, "Here is a red rose. A red rose represents love, so when you see and smell it, you should feel love radiate through your body." In the preceding example, this cookbook approach does indeed describe the experience of the first person. Using that same cookbook protocol with the second person would actually take her away from her true feelings and limit her growth.

To add to this example, suppose these two people come into the same shop five years later and once again see a red rose. They might have completely different reactions based on what they are feeling at this point in their lives. The first person might have lost the love of his life and feel sadness when he sees and smells the red rose. The second person might have gotten over the grief of losing her friend and come to feel the red rose as a symbol of their friendship; so, she might now be the one who feels love when she sees and smells the rose. Once again, the cookbook protocol regarding a red rose and its meaning applies to one person and not the other, although each sees and smells the same red rose.

This preceding example is intended to help you see that applying protocols to your sensations will actually limit your own process of uncovering your true self. The path to uncovering your true self is connecting with what you are feeling in the moment and using those feelings to guide you to your own truth in that moment. So, rather than looking somewhere outside of yourself, seeking what other people say you ought to notice about what you are feeling, you turn inside instead and feel your way to your own truth. To do this, you need to be willing to let go of beliefs about and definitions of "the way things should be"— beliefs which you have acquired or taken on in your life—and instead tune in to what your experiences truly feel like and mean *to you.*

As you continue to read, keep in mind I have made generalizations here to help you understand that everything is interconnected: mind, body, spirit, emotional and physical sensations, perceptions, beliefs, etc. Remember, all of these aspects of experience—aspects we were taught are separate— are actually interconnected and also are unique to each person. In some examples, I describe how particular physical and emotional sensations have been related in various peoples' lives. These examples are just to show you connections that may help with your healing process. On your journey, you might resonate with some of them and not with others. Take them simply as examples to help you with your process, and don't try to change yourself to fit the examples. Occasionally, I also give ideas of what emotions have meant to me, or to others with whom I have worked, only to suggest ideas of what emotions might mean. All the examples and ideas are here to help you to open, to go beyond the meanings you have associated with emotions in the past, to let go of past beliefs, and to open up to new discoveries.

Above all, remember the key to becoming present—to becoming whole, real, and authentic—is to let each moment define itself. When you get lost in past definitions and beliefs, or when you accept others' definitions of how things should be related, you get caught in the protocol, or the cookbook, mentality. That mentality leads you to limit the dynamic process of uncovering your true self. Instead, consider the guidance and ideas others may offer. Then, take only whatever you need from their guidance and ideas to help you uncover what is true for you.

Chapter 7

## Why Do We Need to Listen?

Listening to your body—that is, feeling into the sensations of your body—seems to be the opposite of what most of us have been taught to do. Most methods for physical healing and personal growth seem to promote thinking as our means to heal and grow. This approach teaches us to discount, cover up, modify, or stop what we are feeling. So why would I suggest the means to uncovering your true self is learning to connect into what you are feeling and learning the language of your body?

To begin, take some time to consider your body's truly deep wisdom. Look at how much the body does without our conscious thought, how many important functions of our health are run by this inner-wisdom, by the subconscious. So much happens without our conscious thought: the beating of our heart; the digestion and distribution of our food; the maintaining and rebuilding of our cells; the distribution of blood and oxygen throughout our body; the response to cellular damage or viruses; and on and on. Just think about how amazing, how smart, our body is to keep all these systems functioning and interacting. It is astonishing that the body knows how to distribute the chemicals needed to help repair damaged tissues. We don't need to think about breathing or about converting the food we eat into nutrition for our body. We don't have to consciously make our heart beat. This is all done subconsciously, and luckily so, because if we did have control over these activities, we would probably make a mess of it!

The body knows what it needs and it knows how to heal itself. When the body needs help, it uses physical sensations as a way to get that help. For instance, working in a bent over position (in front of a computer or in a garden) can cause stress to the muscles or joints in your body. As this stress builds, the body triggers the brain to recognize that if the stress continues, the body may be damaged. The body sends a signal— in this example, tension or pressure—to relay the message that there is potential for damage. If we don't listen to this message, the stress continues to build and the signal gets louder, becoming a dull ache. If the pressure continues to build, the signal gets still louder, becoming pain. The body is trying to prevent itself from being injured by sending increasingly louder signals. If the pressure continues, the result could be anything from a muscle strain to a bulging or herniated disc.

If you have had a serious trauma—a car accident, surgery, child birth, a fall—your body might have significant damage. This damage causes restrictions throughout the entire body. Unfortunately, most healthcare professionals are taught to segment the body; they look at only one part of the body, rather than looking at it as a whole. Because of this, many people have significant and unaddressed tissue damage. In such cases, the body uses sensations to try to guide us to a solution, to guide us to where it needs help to regain its health. When we look at these sensations as a guidance system, as an alarm system, instead of as just an annoyance, we can connect into the wisdom of the body and help it to return to balance and health.

Emotional sensations are also part of the guidance system of the body and spirit. Unfortunately, many of us were taught that emotions must be mastered and controlled, or that they are a nuisance and a bother.

Because of what we're typically taught to believe about emotions, we haven't learned how to hear them and to listen to what they are trying to tell us. We haven't realized our true emotions can help us connect to and communicate with our spirit or our guidance. We aren't able to hear or listen to the guidance that is within us. This leads most of us to act in ways that are against our true self. We generally respond according to our programming, steered by beliefs we were taught to hold, thoughts we were taught to think, things we were taught ought to be meaningful to our lives. Acting according to this programming, we miss out on the true happiness we can experience in life.

As we learn to listen to our emotions as guidance, we can start to live from our own truth instead of from what we were taught to think. Emotions are extremely important for guiding each of us to uncovering our true self. As we learn to feel and to connect into them, we can use our emotions to distinguish between what comes from our false self and from our true self. In the next chapter, I offer an exercise that can help you actually feel how the body responds to a truth and to a lie. Feeling these is quite simple once you become aware of each of them. Recognizing and using this physical response will be a valuable tool in your growth process. It can help you to make decisions based on what is true to your spirit instead of on what everyone else thinks you should do. Being true to your spirit is what leads to your empowerment!

## Chapter 8

## *How Do We Listen?*

To be able to listen, you need to learn to be still and to be open to hearing and feeling the things we generally try, or have been taught, not to hear and feel. When we were very young, the mind, body, and spirit all connected quite freely and we knew how to listen and respond to what we felt and heard. We were guided by our emotions, our physical sensations, and our true self. As I discussed in the first chapter, as we got older and went through the process of thinking and categorizing, instead of feeling and going with the flow of life, we shut down this connection and in turn lost access to an amazing guidance system.

Consider this example of how you might have lost your connection with your innate guidance and so with your true self. Part of your programming likely included being taught that eating happens at certain times, according to the beliefs of your family or community, instead of happening according to when you are hungry. Some of you probably followed a very strict schedule: eat breakfast at six, lunch at twelve, and dinner at six, and that's all there was to it. It didn't matter if you were hungry or not; you were taught those are the times at which people eat. Of course, this approach ignored the body's cycles and taught you to disconnect from your body's needs. This scheduled approach went against the instincts to which you responded when you were young: eat when you're hungry and stop when you're full. Our instincts lead us to eat when we need to maintain our bodies; our programming teaches us to eat according to a schedule, regardless of whether we are hungry. Programming about eating often includes the "clean plate" philosophy: you clean your plate no matter what. This teaches kids to override the body's signal telling them they have eaten enough, which can easily lead to overeating and obesity.

When we override the body's wisdom—wisdom focused on survival and health—by following our thoughts and beliefs, those thoughts and beliefs can cause us to be unhealthy. This is what can happen if we decide what, how much, and when to eat by following what we have been taught, instead of listening to our body's wisdom. Becoming disconnected from this aspect of body wisdom can have other unhealthy effects. As we get used to eating without the prompting of our instincts, we may also start to use food to fill an emptiness we feel inside, or as a way to find pleasure, instead of eating because we need energy or nutrients.

This same kind of disconnection can happen with each of the other ways the body or spirit tries to communicate with the mind. Our spirit and body constantly send information to help us maintain their health. We often ignore this information because have been taught to think our way through our experience, rather than connecting with and trusting our feelings and our wisdom to guide us through experience. We think about what or why we should eat, instead of tuning in and asking what our body needs. We think about which emotions are appropriate, and which are not, for each situation, instead of allowing whatever we feel to be okay. We analyze and research, based on income or on what our family or friends think, to determine which job would be the best for us, instead of searching for a profession that will fulfill our spirit. Think of examples from your own life; these examples are here to give you an idea of how we tend to steadily disconnect from our body and spirit, shifting our focus more and more to the logic of the mind.

To have balance in yourself and in your life, you need to have a balance between spirit, body, and mind. The mind isn't bad and neither is using its logic; however, to live your life to the fullest extent, you need to balance the mind and its activities with the spirit and the body and their activities. For overall health, you need to be able to reconnect to the wisdom of your spirit and body and combine that with the logic of your mind. The focus in the modern world seems to be largely on the mind, which causes an imbalance. The body and spirit talk to us all the time, sending us guidance, but we either ignore the guidance or don't know how to listen anymore. It's almost as if the mind, body, and spirit speak different languages. Taking the time to rediscover these different languages, and to help them all meld into one common language, will be a big component in furthering your growth and in connecting to your authentic self.

The following exercises can help you understand how you can use your body's sensations to heal the body itself and to guide you to knowing your own truth. You can do these exercises separately or together.

### *Exercise 1: Getting Comfortable with Feeling*

Before starting, be sure you will have 10 or 15 minutes without being disturbed. Find a place to lie down that's comfortable and quiet. Next, take some time to let your body soften and sink into the surface. After you've softened, you're ready to begin the process of getting comfortable with feeling. Each time you inhale, feel a different part of your body. You can start at the feet and work up, or at the head and work down, or go in any order you want. As you connect with each part of your body, become aware of how it feels. Is there any pain, tension, tightness? Does it feel soft or hard? Don't do anything about it; just feel. As you exhale, let that part of your body soften and let your body sink deeper into the surface where you are lying.

Breathe in—feel.
Breathe out—let go.

Whenever you feel a part or an area that is uncomfortable, your first instinct may be to withdraw your awareness from that place or to try to become more comfortable. Instead of either of these, continue to be aware of the feelings in your body. These sensations are the way the body communicates. The body often uses uncomfortable feelings as a way to draw your awareness to an area that needs help. Bringing your breath into the area and staying present to the sensations is a way to say to your body, "I hear you."

As you continue to breathe into the area that is tight or uncomfortable, get a sense of what the tissue in that area looks like. Is it shaped like a rope, a knot, a cord? Is it smooth or tangled? If a place seems tangled or knotted, visualize it becoming smooth and soft. Does a particular place feel as if it has a color? Don't try to figure it out; just observe. Does the color seem healthy or not? If the color seems healthy, see if you can let the color spread. If it seems unhealthy, see if you can use your breath to bring in a more healthy color to replace it.

If you find a place that is tight or tense, it can be helpful to remind the body that it is safe now. Wherever the body is injured or otherwise traumatized, it tightens to protect these places and to promote their healing. Sometimes, even after the body has healed, the tightness, or bracing, persists. So, when tightness is held in the body as a subconscious bracing pattern, you can help it release by connecting to it consciously.

If a part of your body remains tense or braced after you have followed the steps in this exercise, it needs additional help to soften. For instance, suppose you feel tightness, tension, or pain in an area. You connect with the area, staying present to the sensations you feel, breathing into it, and giving it permission to soften. After you take these steps, the area remains unchanged. In such a case, bodywork may help the area release its tightness, tension, or pain. I will discuss this approach later in the section on applying universal principles to the body.

Doing this exercise—quieting down, connecting, and feeling into the body—is how you can start to communicate with your body. The body talks with sensations. When you realize the sensations you have been trying to avoid are actually the body's way of guiding you to healing, you gain a powerful tool for your healing journey.

Review of steps for this exercise:

1. Get in a comfortable position.
2. Connect into your body.
3. Listen to your body, feeling whatever sensations are present.
4. Be with your body.

Give your body permission to soften, release. Let your body know it is safe and supported.

### *Exercise 2: Moving with Awareness*

Moving with awareness is another way to connect to your body's needs. Developing awareness is what this book is about throughout. The exercises focus specifically on developing awareness, on becoming aware of the guidance we are always being given, guidance we have learned to ignore or forgotten how to interpret. A variety of practices can help increase awareness through movement. For example, some forms of yoga and tai chi can help increase your awareness of your body. However, if you can get moving without following any formal protocol, you can really let your body guide and move you in ways that can actually bring you even more insights than you get with formal movement protocols like yoga or tai chi.

You can do the following exercise in whatever position you feel is most comfortable: sitting, lying, or standing. This one can be great in water! To begin, take a few deep breaths and feel yourself connected to the surface on which you are resting. If you are sitting, feel yourself connected to the chair; if you are standing, feel your feet connected to the ground; and so on. Let yourself really connect with your body and all the sensations you feel. Next, see if you feel your body begin to move on its own. If it doesn't, then initiate a slow movement. It doesn't matter in which direction you go but you want to make three-dimensional, non-linear movements. If you initiate movement, do so very slowly; start reaching, turning, twisting, shifting your weight, allowing your body to move in all directions. Let go of the thought of obtaining a certain position or pose. Let the movements be spontaneous and slow. Let your body explore and express through movement.

Your body is connected head to toe three-dimensionally with connective tissue called the fascia. So, as you move, imagine this three-dimensional elastic tissue expanding and moving. It should have give like that of a knit sweater. It should give up to a point and then reach a stopping point. This stopping point should be gentle. As you move, you may notice some places feel tighter than others. Some places may have a hard or sudden stopping point instead of a smooth end point. Other places may feel completely knotted up and have no give at all. These are areas in your body that need help. If the tissue can't move freely and easily, it causes compression and stress that can lead to dysfunction and pain.

Feeling where tissue is restricted gives you an idea of the places that need to be treated and freed up for your body to work as efficiently as possible. If you have pain, feeling tissue restrictions can help you get an idea of what places may be causing your pain. Feeling within your body with awareness, either when still or when moving, is a way you can start to find out how your body is put together and how you can actually start helping yourself heal. This is a step in empowering yourself, in becoming your own guide instead of giving up your power to others so they can try to "fix" you. You can discover many ways to listen to your own body. The keys are bringing your awareness further into your body; listening to the sensations you find there; letting those sensations help guide you on your personal path to healing and growth.

### *Exercise 3: Feeling Your Truth Detector*

This is an exercise to help you start to answer for yourself, "What is *my* truth?" Begin by lying down in a comfortable position. Follow the steps from the first exercise for quieting down and letting your body settle completely into the surface on which you are lying. Take a few minutes to let your body soften and, as it softens, get an idea of your body's resting tension level. As you breathe and feel into your body, say something you know is a truth. For example, you might say, "I love _____." Fill in the blank with the name of someone you dearly and truly love, or with an activity, a song, a movie, a book you love. As you say these words, feel your body's response to your speaking a truth. Feel for any change in the muscles in your body. Do this several times.

Next, tell yourself a lie about the same topic you used when you spoke your truth. For example, use the sentence again, "I love _____." But this time, fill in the blank with a lie. Tell yourself you love something you actually do not love; to get the biggest response, use something or someone you really dislike at this time. Feel your body's response as you try to convince yourself of a lie. Typically, when you try to convince yourself of something you know isn't true, you will feel some part of your body become tense or tight. It might be any part of your body. What tightens in you may be different from what tightens in other people; don't compare yourself with others. This is about finding out what works for you. Do this several times. Don't worry if you don't feel something right away. Sometimes it can be very subtle. Just play with it.

After you identify your "lie detector," start to use it in your life. So you don't put yourself under any pressure, start to experiment with your lie detector by using it with small, relatively inconsequential things at first. For example, the next time you go to the store, stop in the produce department and ask yourself, "What fruit do I want to eat?" Name the various fruits to yourself and see which one feels like the truth for you. For instance, as you say "strawberries," you may feel your body responding like it does when you say a truth. So, in this instance, your truth is your body wants strawberries.

As the next part of your experiment with feeling truth, see what your mind does with a truth you've felt. In our example in the produce department, once you find a fruit that feels like a truth to you, notice how your mind behaves. Do you instantly start negating your truth? For instance, does your mind say, "Yes, but... strawberries don't last long and they are expensive, so I should really get apples." If you follow your truth, you will enjoy the strawberries. If you follow your mind, you may find yourself looking at the apples a week later and saying to yourself, "I really didn't want the apples. I wanted strawberries. My mind talked me out of what my body wanted." As you experiment with your lie detector, once you've felt a truth, if your mind doesn't try to negate it, see how you feel if you deliberately try to talk yourself out of your truth.

If you begin using your lie detector with small things, there really isn't a lot at stake. This is a great way to start noticing when you listen to your truth or guidance, when you talk yourself out of it, and how both of those feel to you. As you practice feeling truth, you can begin trusting your true self more on bigger, more important issues, issues like whether to buy a particular house, to get married, to change jobs. If we never listen with the small things, how can we expect to be able to have clear guidance on the bigger issues? Play with it. Ask in all aspects: "What clothes do I want to wear? What movie do I want to see? What do I want to eat?" The more you practice what it feels like to feel truth and what it feels like to negate that truth, the easier it will be for you to listen to your guidance. As you do this more and more, notice how often you listen to your guidance and how often you let yourself be talked out of what you really want.

You may find these exercises difficult because each involves quieting down and feeling what is inside you. This can be difficult if you have been taught you shouldn't feel anything uncomfortable. Believing we shouldn't feel discomfort is why so many people get caught up in a frantic pace of life. So many of us don't stop, don't slow down, don't experience quiet. There's generally radio, TV, or something else to distract us. We distract ourselves so we don't have to feel the things inside of us that are uncomfortable and we don't know how to handle.

Because we are trying so hard not to feel, we use medications to dull ourselves and then need other medications to give us energy. This is why so many people use drugs all day long. So many people start the day with caffeine, get themselves through the day with more medicines, and then end the day with a drink or something else to get themselves shut down. More and more people are taking over-the-counter and prescribed pills to keep themselves at a constant state because they don't want to feel low at any time. Consequently, they don't feel the highs anymore either. They can no longer feel the joy or the passion for life.

The preceding exercises, and the other ones in this book, are here to help you connect into the uncomfortable feelings so you can use them as guidance in healing. One of the primary reasons we avoid being still and feeling is we don't know what to do with uncomfortable sensations, physical, emotional, or otherwise. As a result, these feelings build up until they are all we feel. They become overwhelming and so the only option is to shut down. Use the exercises as an effective way to bring up your uncomfortable feelings; then, feel them, release them, and reclaim your true self.

The exercises in this book are a great way to start on the path of feeling, releasing, and reclaiming. As you practice them, you will likely feel some areas release physically and may also feel some emotions come up. As you bring in your awareness and let these sensations out, you will feel more space and ease. Along the way in this book, I describe some approaches to using bodywork to release physical restrictions, as well as emotions, beliefs, and thoughts.

Chapter 9

*Physical Sensations*

When someone is asked the question "How does your body communicate with you?" the most common response is "Pain." It seems pain and the avoidance of it have become the main focus of healthcare. We have been taught pain is bad and should be avoided. We learn that if we can't avoid pain, we ought to have something done to block it, and, if that doesn't work, we ought to be taught how to "live with it."

Pain is certainly one physical sensation, but there are many others. Consider some other physical sensations: heat, burning, stretch, vibration, cold, chills, shakes, tingling, pressure, pulling. Any sensation that has some sort of physical implication is a physical sensation. We have generally been taught to avoid, overcome, or ignore unpleasant physical sensations like pain. However, all of the unpleasant physical sensations listed here are examples of how the body communicates its needs. If we learn to recognize these sensations as the body's language, instead of ignoring them, we can harness our body's wisdom to help with true health. These sensations are the body's way of trying to get our attention and also trying to help guide us to what it needs to restore or maintain health.

Let's consider this in completely different way than we normally do. Instead of looking at these sensations as bad or as something to be avoided, try looking at them as an alarm system. Pain, pressure, pulling, and achiness are all ways the body tries to tell us there is something going on the body does not like and is, or soon could be, causing us harm. Usually the body starts with lesser sensations, a little ache, a bit of pressure; most of the time we ignore these sensations and push through them. Why? Many of us have been taught to believe "No pain, no gain" or that being able to endure pain is a sign of being tough. If we do acknowledge the pain, most of us know only to take medicine or do exercises. We do these things to ease or stop the pain, but we do not know what to do to help our body truly heal.

So, we keep pushing on. This is when the sensations get louder. We may begin feeling a deeper ache or a throb. These sensations turn into pain if we do not listen to them. If we continue to ignore the pain, it gets more intense. If we still don't get the messages, the body may start sending the pain to other parts of the body. It's as if the body is saying, "Obviously the owner of this body can't feel the pain in his hip. He can't hear me when I send the message there, so if I send it to the other hip or to the back, maybe he'll hear that I need help." This cycle of the body escalating the pain messages while we ignore them tends to continue until we have so much pain that we are forced to rest, we're forced to stop.

Instead of getting to the point of being forced to stop by escalating pain, try learning to see the uncomfortable or unpleasant physical sensations as guidance rather than as the enemy. These kinds of sensations are our alarm system. Consider a smoke detector as an analogy to physical sensations like pain. A smoke detector's job is to send a signal, an alarm, when it detects smoke. Pain, pressure, pulling—all of these get triggered when there's something wrong in the body. When the body detects too much pressure or force in an area, it determines damage could be caused. So it sends out a signal, just like the smoke detector does when it detects smoke.

When the smoke detector goes off, it doesn't tell you whether it was triggered because there is toast burning in the toaster or because your house is on fire. Its job is simple: if it detects smoke, it alerts you by sending a signal that indicates it has detected smoke. It's your job to go look and find out what's causing the alarm to be triggered—to find the problem—and then to determine the appropriate action. You might need to call the fire department or just to unplug the toaster.

It's the same thing when you have unpleasant or uncomfortable physical sensations (and the same is true of emotional sensations, which I'll discuss in the next chapter). When the alarm system goes off, it's your job to *feel* and find out what's going on. Sometimes you just need to shift your weight, or stop what you're doing, or do a simple stretch. Other times you may need to go see a professional to help your body heal. When you have the mentality that the signal (that is, the pain) is the problem, you miss the fact that you are actually being guided, that something is out of balance and needs help.

Most of the focus in healthcare has been on stopping the signal instead of paying attention to it as a message: "Go find the problem and what is causing it." This would be like walking up to a smoke detector that's going off and putting a pillow over it. If you can't hear the alarm, or if the smoke can't get to the detector to set off the alarm, everything is fine. Right? You can see the problem with this approach. You probably don't want to be standing there with a pillow over the smoke detector while the house burns down around you! If you don't use your sensations as guides, and instead just try to cover up or stop the pain without finding its cause, you could actually cause more damage than good; your body could crumble down around you.

So, try to stop being afraid of the uncomfortable and unpleasant sensations and start using them as guides. Taking this approach, you can become truly empowered in your healing process. We need to be taught to feel these sensations instead of blocking them and then to use them as a guide to the source of the problem. As you practice allowing yourself to feel more and more, you will get better and better at understanding what each sensation means to your body and how your body is connected.

We often decide to get help only when our pain reaches a level that forces us to stop. Getting help may mean seeing a number of practitioners for a variety of treatments; you might see a massage therapist, a physical therapist, a doctor, or some other healthcare practitioner. You can get back on track relatively quickly if you are lucky enough to find someone who knows how to treat the body as a whole and to help the body release. Unfortunately, most of the healthcare practitioners don't approach or treat the body in these ways, having been taught to treat only symptoms.

When I went through physical therapy school, the majority of teaching was done in a way that segmented the body. The shoulder isn't even in the same chapter as the hip and there's no suggestion of those two being connected in some significant way! We were taught specific evaluations based on symptoms: if someone comes in with shoulder pain, address the shoulder; with hip pain, address the hip; with headaches, address the head. There was very little, if any, focus on addressing the body as a whole. We learned to use a particular set of evaluations for a given symptom or group of symptoms. Based on our evaluations, we learned to use a particular protocol of exercises to treat the place where the symptoms were occurring.

The problem with this symptom-focused, body-segmenting, protocol-based approach is it fails to take into account that the entire body is connected. Using what I learned in physical therapy school, I was frequently able to help people by simply treating their symptoms. However, sometimes my treatments helped a patient achieve only partial improvement, not full recovery. This is because I was taught to chase the symptoms instead of finding the source of the problems. Often, a patient I had been treating for a given symptom would come in for a session and have new symptoms in other places; since we weren't taught that the entire body is connected, this just didn't make any sense. Sometimes with some patients, when I treated the symptoms, they actually became worse. Because I, like most of healthcare professionals, was taught to treat symptoms, I hadn't been taught what to do when that approach doesn't work. I had been taught to look at pain as bad and wrong, as something to eliminate, rather than as a guide to help the body return to health.

As with everything you learn along your path, be open to the information guiding you, instead of following someone else's definition of what the information might mean to you. Be open to your immediate sensations and avoid judging them based on what similar sensations may have meant to you in the past. Be open each time. For example, if you have chills, don't assume it means you are cold. Be with the chills for a few breaths and see if you feel more than you did at first. After doing this, you might feel you are simply cold and need more layers of clothing. Perhaps you feel the chills indicating you are on the verge of becoming sick. Or, you might feel those same chills as your body releasing energy.

Remember not to fall into the protocols. Avoid people, books, or any other source of information providing a single definition for a given sensation. For example: cold means this and heat means that; the pain in your knee means you're unable to step forward in your life; the pain in your jaw means you are suppressing anger. Each sensation and each location can have endless possibilities; following protocols can slow down or block your healing. Anyone or anything that tries to give you a cookbook analogy for a sensation or a pain, for a color or a dream, offers nothing useful so far as determining your needs in a given moment.

Let each sensation define itself in the moment. When you are feeling something, breathe, feel, and ask yourself, "What does this sensation mean to me at this moment?" Give yourself time to let the answer come from within you. Most of the time, the first response will be from your head—what you *think* the answer *should be*—so give yourself time for several options to come up. Then, sit with the answers you get and see which one is your truth. This entire process is dynamic by nature. Seeing a butterfly in your dream one day may mean something completely different than what it means on a day four years later. It's all about feeling and asking yourself, "What does this mean to me *right now*, in *this* time?" This is how you start to use your physical sensations to guide you to what your body needs.

# Chapter 10

## *Emotional Sensations*

As I discussed earlier, almost every physical sensation has an emotional component at some level. Why is this? We are often hurt as a result of a trauma or an accident and these experiences usually have some kind of emotional component. For example, suppose you were told as a child not to climb trees and, when you did so anyway (like most kids do!), you fell and broke your arm. When this happens, not only do you have the physical pain of breaking your arm, but you might also think, "They told me I wasn't supposed to climb the tree. I fell out and hurt myself, so I deserve this." Or you might think, "I'm gonna be in so much trouble when they find out!" So, in addition to the physical sensations associated with this injury, you might also feel fear: "What will my parents do when they find out I've done this?!" Emotions can be intertwined with physical sensations. If you do not address the emotions associated with a trauma, if you do not feel or express them in some way, you may prevent yourself from healing.

The healthcare system tends to overlook, dismiss, or avoid emotions. Generally, healthcare professionals are taught to dissect and divide not only the body and the physical sensations, but also the emotional sensations. I divided this section of this book into physical, emotional, and other sensations for teaching purposes alone. You cannot really divide these sensations to understand or treat them, any more than you can divide up the body to understand or treat it. In both cases, this kind of approach does not work.

Emotions serve the same general purpose as physical sensations: they are a guidance system. By acknowledging and addressing the importance of emotional sensations, we make use of a guidance system that can help us on our healing path; by ignoring them, we rob ourselves of that same guidance and the help it can give us. As with the physical sensations, the key with emotional sensations is to feel them fully and to let go of judgments about them. When an emotion comes up, feel it and let go of judging the emotion as good or bad, right or wrong, appropriate or inappropriate for the situation.

We have so many guidelines concerning when and how we should or shouldn't feel. Sticking to these guidelines keeps us from being our real, authentic self. For example, many believe it is appropriate to grieve the death of a loved one. But how is this belief affected when the person you loved died doing something reckless? Perhaps the one you loved drove too fast and got into an accident, sent text while driving, or did something else that leaves you angry, angry she did something that caused her to die. Is it appropriate to feel anger towards someone after their death? If you believe or are told it isn't appropriate, you might push the anger down, which then slows or even stops your healing process. Here's another example of a belief that can limit healing: it's appropriate to grieve deeply over the loss of a child, but when someone in their 80s or 90s dies, that person lived so long you ought to be able to accept the death more easily and not grieve as long. In truth, when someone you love dies, regardless of their age, you need to feel that loss fully and grieve to whatever degree you need to grieve. Another example is the death of a pet. Some people think losing a pet ought to be a small matter; for others, losing a pet can be the same as losing a child. These examples suggest it's essential for you to feel what's appropriate for you in any situation.

Another set of beliefs concerns the circumstances in which it is appropriate to express emotions. At times, it may be imprudent to express your emotions, either fully or perhaps at all. When should you stuff them? Consider an example. Suppose your boss yells at you and you feel angry. If you decide to yell back at your boss, you might lose your job. If you feel you are still supposed to have that job, you need to control the expression of your emotions—somewhat or even completely—at that time.

We all need to suppress emotions at times. The key to choosing to suppress emotions is what you do afterwards. Do you give yourself time to express those emotions in an appropriate manner? Do you have a punching bag, pillow, or other object you use to let out the stored up emotions and clear them from your body? If you don't, if you keep stuffing emotions and letting them build, the next thing you know you find yourself involved in a road rage incident. Or you will go home and take it out on your spouse, child, or pet. If you have stored up enough anger, it may even turn into an abusive situation. Remember: an emotion is neither bad nor good, but what you do with the emotion—when, where, and how you chose to express it—can be either appropriate or inappropriate, and can lead to either helping or harming yourself or others.

Some of the many other commonly-held beliefs about emotions may have affected or still be affecting your life. A pretty common belief is that girls and boys should have different emotional responses to a given situation. Another is that emotions are somehow age-appropriate; based on your age, you should or shouldn't express certain emotions. Some believe emotions shouldn't be expressed to strangers. The list of emotional rules seems like it could go on and on, and it varies based on your family, community, geographical region, and country. It can feel impossible to keep up with the changes in the rules. This leads many people to shut down emotionally as a way of trying to stay within the rules: if you don't express any emotion, you might avoid breaking the rules.

Becoming aware of your beliefs and discerning which ones are true to you and which are harmful, you can begin choosing to keep the healthy beliefs and to change or replace the harmful ones. Stuffing emotions and shutting down can eventually cause you to do things that could harm others or yourself. Instead, you can start to notice when you stuff, shut down, or overreact, and then choose another option. This approach allows you to stay centered and present in your current situation.

How do you know you have stuffed emotions? You find yourself overreacting to a situation. Someone says or does something mildly annoying or irritating and your reaction is way above and beyond the intensity of the other person's comment or action. You just lose it, literally—you lose your emotions and they spill out all over the place. Your overreaction could come out as anger, sadness, frustration, hurt, or any other emotion. If you find yourself overreacting, you know you have a buildup of emotions and it's time to find a way to connect with and release them. The key to detecting stuffed emotions, as it has been in the other instances I've discussed so far, is to increase your awareness by letting yourself feel. Notice when you are reacting and notice when you are feeling what is real in the moment. Learn to recognize when your emotions are building up so you can release them instead of letting them continue to build. This will allow you to become more fully alive and present in the moment.

The next segment of this chapter concerns beliefs and feelings about various emotions. It begins with an exercise to help you discover any hidden beliefs and feelings you have about emotions. In the remainder of this segment, I discuss a number of specific emotions one by one. At the end of the discussion of each emotion, I suggest some of the possible benefits of having the emotion and some of the possible limitations or pitfalls from having it. Following each discussion is an exercise to help you discover any hidden beliefs and feelings you have about that emotion.

In discussing each emotion, I'm raising just some of the possibilities in a dynamic system. You may resonate with some of the examples I give and not with others; take what you need and leave the rest. The discussions and exercises are simply a way to help you become aware of your beliefs and feelings about emotions. You may find you want to expand on the benefits or the limitations and pitfalls of a given emotion based on your beliefs and on what you are feeling or experiencing in the moment. The discussions and exercises are **not** a protocol establishing a specific meaning for a given emotion. Rather, they provide some examples from which you can expand based on your own beliefs and experiences. It's about finding what feels right for you. Be open to look at your beliefs in a new perspective. See which beliefs are beneficial and which ones might be limiting your healing or your being authentic. Nothing will stop your progress faster than a closed mind!

### *Exercise: Uncovering Beliefs and Feelings about Various Emotions*

To begin, get in a comfortable position and let yourself really soften into the surface on which you are resting. Let yourself feel safe and supported. Let your body soften.

Next, you will ask yourself some questions having to do with emotions. As you do so, let go of the need to have an answer come up. Let go of the need for answers to come in the form of words. Just be open to whatever comes up. You may have words or phrases come up, emotions, colors... you may see flashes of scenes from your life or from movies you have seen. Ask yourself these questions—and others that occur to you as you go—with curiosity. Let go of any judgments. Just let yourself feel and be guided. Take time with each question. As you allow yourself time to feel in response to a question, you may have several different emotions, words, scenes, or other responses come up.

I suggest asking yourself the following questions to help you uncover your beliefs and feelings about various emotions. These are examples of questions to help in this process. Expand on these questions and ask others that occur to you, as you feel appropriate; however, avoid the "why" questions. Questions that begin with "why" lead you to try to think of a solution logically instead of being guided to the truth. Take your time with each question. Give yourself several minutes with each question. You'll find it helpful to journal about what comes up for you.

Now, ask yourself these questions:

- What is the worst that would happen if I cried?

- What have I been taught about the expression of anger?

- When was the first time I learned it wasn't appropriate to be happy?

- Where did I get the belief that I should never be afraid?

As you work with these questions, try substituting any emotion or expression of an emotion.

As the last question you pose yourself, ask: What is a healthier belief about the expression of [any emotion you choose]?

Take time to revisit these questions along your healing journey. Your answers will continue to change as your life experience changes. This isn't about establishing a fixed belief. It's about revisiting your beliefs continuously to see which ones are helpful and which ones may be harmful or limiting to your growth.

Now we move on to address some specific emotions one by one. As you read the discussion of each emotion, remember: emotions aren't wrong, they're not bad or good, they just are. Emotions are simply an expression of energy. It's not the emotion that is bad; we can create a problem when we suppress the emotion and then it comes out in a harmful way. The emotion does not cause a problem; what we do, or don't do, with it does.

**Anger, irritation, frustration, agitation, rage**

Anger—especially in its extreme: rage—is typically labeled a "bad" emotion. Many people actually fear feeling anger and are afraid of others feeling it. Anger is often thought of as an emotion we should neither see nor express because it is associated with hurting others. As with all emotions, anger is not actually bad or wrong—it simply *is*; it is an expression, a manifestation, of energy.

You don't have to look far to find unhealthy beliefs about and expressions of anger. For example, consider the person who is so afraid of anger or of upsetting others that they don't set boundaries and they let people walk all over them. Or, consider people, children and adults alike, who have been in abusive situations in which they see anger leading to hurt. Because they haven't seen how emotions can be expressed in a positive manner, those who have witnessed or experienced abuse are often the ones that have the hardest time expressing anger. They tend to suppress their anger until they end up doing the very thing they said they would never do: striking out in anger. Someone who has witnessed or experienced abuse often becomes an abuser—the one thing they said they would never be—because, not taught how to express it appropriately, they so fear and suppress their anger that it builds up until it explodes in a harmful manner. This is how the cycle of anger and abuse gets passed on.

What is an appropriate way to express anger? When you experience anger, what should you do with it? That depends on the situation. As I suggested earlier, sometimes you may decide it is inappropriate or unwise to express anger at the moment you feel it. Recall the example of being angry at your boss and deciding not to express it so as to avoid the chance of losing your job at that moment. However, each situation is unique. At another time when you are angry at your boss, you might decide to express it at that moment because you truly feel you need to change your work situation. It can be very appropriate to express your anger to the person who upset you; it may even be needed and beneficial, as when it is time to set a boundary or change a situation. The Mothers Against Drunk Drivers (MADD) campaign is an example of an appropriate, beneficial, and needed expression of anger: anger over the loss of a child led to establishing an organization aimed at preventing similar situations.

If you find yourself in a situation in which you become angry and choose not to express the anger, you need to find a way to release it that is appropriate and works for you. Releasing delayed or suppressed anger—anger you chose not to express at the time you became angry—helps keep you healthy and balanced. It also reduces the likelihood you'll take your anger out on someone else. To release suppressed anger, find or create an appropriate environment and do something to get the energy and the words out. Let the anger go before you get in your car or go home!

Here are some suggestions of ways to release suppressed anger:

- Take a walk.

- Punch a pillow.

- Hit a tree with a stick.

- Jump up and down. (Not a good option on an airplane!)

- Let yourself say whatever you would like to say.

- Yell, scream, kick—do what you need to do to get it out!

One person told me they liked to buy a piñata and smash it up. When you're in an environment appropriate for releasing suppressed anger, it's okay to say and do whatever you feel at the time. You can even pretend you are hitting the person with whom you are angry; this is a way to get it out of you so you won't end up actually hitting that person. These are examples of ways to dispel the anger that are not only appropriate, but also often lead you to clearing old anger you didn't even know you had built up. Remember it's not the emotions that are bad. Emotions usually cause problems because we weren't taught to express them appropriately or to deal with them in a healthy manner.

*Some possible benefits of anger:* Anger can lead to: action; setting boundaries; making changes in your life or changes that can benefit an entire family, country, or the world. This emotion can be channeled for positive growth and action.

*Some possible limitations or pitfalls of anger*: If anger is stuffed down instead of being expressed appropriately, it can lead to causing harm to yourself or others. Recall the example of the person who gets yelled at while at work and then lets the anger build to the point where they let the anger out in a hurtful manner when they get home. Watch out for righteous anger. In righteous anger, a person feels entitled to be angry and views that anger as justification for hurting or killing others. "They did this, so they deserve to be punished." Even great causes can turn into a disaster when righteous anger becomes involved. For example, when people in Greenpeace ram their boat into other boats, they take action that can hurt or kill other people. Righteous anger is often involved when people justify murdering those who have a different skin color, different beliefs, or faith in another religion. Righteous anger can turn you into the very thing you started fighting against.

### Exercise: Uncovering Beliefs and Feelings about Anger and Its Variants

Take some time now to uncover some of your beliefs about anger. Quiet yourself down and ask, "What is the worst that could happen if I expressed anger? What are my beliefs about anger and rage?" You may find many different beliefs and feelings come up; allow this to happen and take the opportunity to journal about what comes up. Then, ask, "What is a more healthy way to view anger now?" Again, be open to, and journal about, whatever comes up. Also be open to letting your answers evolve as you go through your life. Your answers will change as you learn more throughout your life.

### Sadness, sorrow, grief

Sadness and its variants are also emotions often feared, avoided, or labeled as "bad." When you have had any kind of loss in your life, expressing your sadness and grieving is a path that leads to healing. Losses come in many forms: loss of a family member, friend, or other loved one; loss of physical ability (through age, injury, accident, stroke, etc.); loss of a dream, belief, or idea of how things "should be" in your life; loss of a job or a house; loss of a relationship. After a loss of any kind, it is only through feeling the sadness, going through the grieving process, that we eventually move to acceptance and healing. Think of the tears that fall when you are grieving as being like rain—they bring forth new growth. The tears are a way for your heart and soul to cleanse themselves of the pain of losing things no longer a part of your life; the tears help you prepare for new opportunities to come into your life. Repressed sadness can build up just like anger. If you stuff down sadness, over time, it can lead to depression and to loss of joy. If your body is full of sadness, it has no room for joy.

Many beliefs can hinder you from feeling and expressing sadness. You may have been told you aren't supposed to cry, that doing so is a sign of weakness. You may have been taught there is an appropriate length of time for sadness, after which "you should be over it." You may have been told, "Stop crying, or I will give you something to cry about." You usually hear this when you are expressing a hurt in your heart; this statement teaches you crying is only appropriate when you have physical injury or pain. You may also have been taught that even if you are sad, you are supposed to put on the happy face and pretend that everything is alright. Your role in your family might have been the one who keeps everyone else uplifted, and so you can't be sad or express sadness. These are a few examples; you can probably think of many other beliefs about sadness and its expression.

*Some possible benefits of sadness, sorrow, grief*: These emotions can lead to healing. By expressing your sadness, sorrow, or grief, you can clear and cleanse your heart which will then lead to an opening. By feeling and expressing these emotions, you can be led to healing and to creating space for new life and love to come into your life. Sadness can also be a signal you need to make a change in your life.

*Some possible limitations or pitfalls of sadness, sorrow, grief*: If you do not express these emotions, then they can build up and lead to prolonged depression and the loss of joy and love in your life. A pitfall can be getting stuck in the cycle of sadness and not moving to the clearing or opening that allows for new opportunities to enter your life.

### Exercise: Uncovering Beliefs and Feelings about Sadness and Its Variants

Just as you did with anger, take some time now and ask, "What would be the worst thing that could happen if I cried or expressed sadness?" Be with this question awhile and give yourself time for various answers to come up. Feel the emotions associated with these beliefs. As with all emotions, you need to find a way to express sorrow that feels right to *you.* We are afraid of "losing control." The truth is we are really good at controlling our emotions, in fact, too good for our own good! Controlling and suppressing our emotions leads to so many of our problems.

A fear I have heard so many people express (and one that I have had too) is that if they start crying, they will never stop. To help quiet this fear, try giving yourself a time frame. For instance, decide you will really let yourself go into your emotions for 10 or 15 minutes; have a clock nearby so you can check the time. (This same approach works for all emotions.) Give yourself permission to go really deeply into the sadness, sorrow, hurt, loss, etc. Make this time an opportunity to go inside and clear space. Allow yourself to really feel to the depths of your emotions, and then clear the space they occupied. When you do this, you free yourself to feel other emotions… like happiness!

When the time is up, take a few deep breaths and feel the space you created. What you do with this space is up to you. You might just want to enjoy the feeling of the space. Or, you might want to do something to fill that space with love, joy, happiness. You can breathe colors or feelings into the new space. You might decide it's a good time to do something that helps you feel happiness or joy: take a walk, play with a pet or a child, go to a museum, drink a cup of tea—anything you enjoy. It doesn't have to be anything big, just something that brings you a sense of joy, contentment, quiet, or happiness.

Sometimes, people go into full blown depression because they've suppressed sadness for so long that they can feel only the very emotions they have been trying not to feel. They no longer have any space open to let in joy and happiness. In this case, your body, heart, and spirit are so clogged up with hurt, sadness, and sorrow they can't feel love anymore. So, it seems all there is in your life is sadness. Even when it's a beautiful day and you are surrounded by people and things you love, all you can feel is the sadness. The body and spirit want you to feel and clear these emotions, emotions that are suffocating you. If you have been taught or believe you shouldn't feel sad, you don't give yourself the opportunity to feel and clear your sadness. To create this opportunity, start by letting yourself feel into the sadness for just a breath or two. From there, practice increasing the time you allow yourself to feel. Soon, you will start to realize feeling the emotions leads to healing. It often takes time to get comfortable feeling the emotions that make you uncomfortable, just as it does with getting comfortable feeling the physical sensations that make you uncomfortable.

*A note about medication for depression:*

Medications that keep you from feeling should be used only in extreme cases of depression. Such medications lead to further suppression of feeling, which in turn adds to the depression. When medicine is necessary, your most effective goal is to use it until you can clear enough to be able to come off the medicine. The goal with any medicine designed to help relieve a symptom—whether physical or emotional— should be temporary use while you work to regain your balance, at which time you no longer need the medicine.

Sadness can also signal the need for change of some kind. If you feel a lot of sadness and grief and despair, maybe it's time for a life change. Maybe it's time for creating space in your life for some joy, but you won't know this until you feel the sadness fully and sit with it. If you find yourself running from one situation to the next and the sadness stays, you're getting a signal that you need to look inside yourself. Start to notice your patterns. If the situations change, but the emotions and outcomes stay the same, look at the common denominator: you. In this case, it's not about changing the external circumstances—"It's that person's fault, or it's my job, or if I just moved to another part of the country...," etc.—it's about healing what's internal.

Just like with anger, when you are extremely emotional, when any little thing seems to get you upset or make you very sad or depressed, your body is telling you there's some sadness or grief in you that needs to be felt. Take the time to let yourself feel into what has you upset. Really let yourself feel it, feeling beyond the current situation into all the times you have felt this same way. And again, as with anger, after you have gone in and felt your way to some space, take time to appreciate the space that's been created. At this point you might want to feel some things for which you are grateful or that you love and let those feelings into your body. Creating space will help break free from the hold of depression. You will no longer feel trapped in the sadness and sorrow and will have room for life. If you can't pull yourself out, try going in even deeper until you eventually break through to the other side. Take time to do things that bring joy into your life. By taking control, going into your sadness, and creating space, you will start to empower your healing.

**Fear, panic, anxiety, terror, nervousness**

What is the purpose of fear? In its true form, fear is an emotion or signal that can help save your life. It can provide energy, a burst of adrenaline, in case we need to use our fight-or-flight response. It's for protection, survival, and warning. Peter Levine's insightful book *Waking the Tiger* discusses the purposes of fear and how to deal with fear's many levels.

Fear can become a problem too. One way this can happen is if you fail to dispel the energy generated by the fear of a real threat once that threat is over or gone. When you're in a real life-or-death situation, you experience a rush of adrenaline that gives you the ability to act quickly. Adrenaline gives you a tremendous burst of energy for a short term response, for instance, fighting, running, or lifting something very heavy. Once you are safe or determine your reaction was a false alarm, you need to dispel any energy remaining from the adrenaline rush. Animals do this naturally. When an animal senses a possible danger, its body becomes tense and adrenaline surges into the blood in case it needs to act. If the animal realizes its response was a false alarm, it shakes its body, yawns, stomps, or does something else to dispel the energy. While other animals do this freely, we humans rarely do it at all and so the energy tends to stay locked in our bodies.

Another way fear can become a problem is if you have constant fear or anxiety from a danger you create in your mind. This kind of danger is called a perceived threat. When you perceive the stresses of life as a threat, you experience constant worry and anxiety; you're not really in a life-or-death situation, but your mind perceives the stresses of life as threatening. Examples of this kind of fear are worrying constantly about your to-do list or feeling anxiety constantly from trying to crunch 10 hours' worth of tasks into 4 hours. A perceived threat is a constant stress that makes your body feel like it's actually being threatened. The body responds to a perceived threat just as seriously as a real threat.

The fight-or-flight response is a natural, fear-driven reaction to a serious threat. When threatened seriously, we react by either fighting or fleeing. The fight-or-flight response is to last a relatively short time, just long enough to eliminate the threat of danger. If you are stuck in a cycle of fight-or-flight for hours, days, months, or years, you may experience fatigue, exhaustion, and even systemic disorders. Your body isn't designed to sustain the fight-or-flight response. To dispel the energy of this kind of response, you need to let yourself feel and express. Let yourself go into your doubts, fears, and anxieties. Ask yourself, "What is the worst that can happen?" "What am I most afraid could happen?" Obviously, if you are in a real life-or-death situation, you need to act immediately. In some circumstances, you need to feel the fear and then react so you remain safe.

When you are caught in the cycle of going through the "worst case scenario" over and over in your head, you cause fear and anxiety with your own thoughts. In this situation, you create all kinds of scenarios about what might happen and usually find yourself imagining the extremes. For example, you might take a simple thing like walking from a parking lot into a restaurant and turn it into a scene from a horror movie. When you park your car in the lot, you're feeling happy. You're going to meet your friends to have a nice dinner and then to listen to a band. As you shut off your car, you notice there isn't anyone else in the parking lot. It's dark and you have to walk past an alleyway to get to the restaurant. Now, is this a real fear or a perceived fear? It might be either, or some of both. True fear comes from your gut. If you notice your mind creating all kinds of images based on all the crime television you have been watching lately, then the fear is from your head. If you have flashes of characters from all the horror movies you have ever seen coming out and attacking you, then it's your mind going overboard. Before you know it, you are too scared to even get out of your car.

This is how fears can paralyze you. Even when you create fear in your mind, your body perceives it as a real threat. The fear still triggers the same physiological responses in your body. If your first fear response is actually triggered by your intuition because there truly is danger, but then your mind takes over with all kinds of extreme scenarios, you may have difficulty distinguishing between the two. This is often what causes people to end up in unsafe situations. They can't tell the difference between the fear that arises for protection and the fear that their mind creates.

Here is a personal example of working with fears. Each day, I walk my dogs in a nature reserve across the road from my house. As the days get shorter with the approach of winter, I find myself walking in the dark more often than not, depending on when I leave on the walk. This has turned out to be a wonderful opportunity to face some of my fears, to trust, and to go with the flow. When I was walking, I noticed most of the time I knew the trails so well I didn't even need to focus on where I was going. So, I thought I would test this out by turning off my flashlight when I began walking in the dark. As soon as I turned off the flashlight, every possible image of monsters, ax murderers, wolves, bears, creatures from *The Lord of the Rings*, even Godzilla himself, started flashing through my head. I felt a paralyzing fear clench around my heart. Even after I turned on the flashlight, it took me several minutes to get myself together. The adrenaline rushed through my body in case I needed to run from or fight these monsters I created in my head. My heart pounded. A voice in my head told me to head back home, now! One minute, I was enjoying a beautiful walk in the woods and the next minute, my irrational fear had taken me over.

This experience really opened my eyes to how much the mind can create fear and stop us in our tracks. It gave me a great opportunity to work with my true fear guidance and with irrational fear, and to learn to feel the difference between the two. So, I started playing around with it. How long could I keep the flashlight off? How far could I walk before I stepped off the trail? Not only was it a test of fear, but also of trust and flow. If I tried to see the trail, I usually couldn't (unless the moon was really bright). If I stopped trying to see the trail and just trusted my feet to guide me, then I stayed on it. Many times my mind doubted the route my feet were taking and was sure I needed to go another way... and that's when I would end up off the trail!

Sometimes I had to turn on the flashlight because of my fears. Other times I turned it on because I didn't trust where I was going. I just let myself observe this without judging or thinking I should do better. If I fought with my mind, then my mind gained more control. If I acknowledged the fears and doubts without investing in them, they lost more and more control and I regained more of my true guidance.

Eventually, I walked several days in a row without feeling like I needed to turn on my flashlight. The next step was leaving the flashlight at home. That was a big step and felt like I was starting over. Without my security blanket to fall back on, the doubts and fears came back strong. Suddenly the dark seemed 10 times darker! This is when another gift occurred. When I got really scared and stopped, one of my dogs would come back and guide me forward on the trail. This was a lesson in trusting and opening up to help. Could I really open up and trust help would be there if I needed it? This experience led me to realize I held a belief that you only get help if you "deserve it," that you need to work hard or do something "special" to receive help. It also helped me realize my reluctance to ask for or to accept help was founded in a belief that needing help means you are weak.

This exercise of walking in the woods in the dark may have started as something to help with my fear of darkness, but it evolved into lessons in my beliefs about trusting, asking for help, and receiving. This is important to note. As you head out in one direction, be open to all the different beliefs that may come up. This is how you keep the healing process authentic and dynamic. Let go of any rigid guidelines.

These walks in the dark woods made me notice how much my irrational fears are not just a part of my life but a controlling force. The walks also helped me get a felt sense of the difference between fear that my mind creates and fear that tries to guide and protect me. Sometimes when I was walking I would get a twinge of fear that felt different from the crazy-monster-fear my mind created. The first time this happened I was walking in the daylight and saw a coyote close by. I didn't feel my life was threatened or anything serious like that, but the coyote could certainly have been a danger to my dogs. Feeling the fear from that real danger, I also had a felt sense of the difference between that kind of fear and the fear from something created in my mind.

*A very important note about my exercise of walking in the woods in the dark:*

I could play around with this because I knew I wasn't in danger. The nature reserve I walk in is small. Even if I got completely lost, I would reach a road or a house within ½ mile maximum in any direction. There aren't any cliffs I could fall off or any other similar dangers if I got off the trail. This is not a place where I walked out into miles of wilderness or into territory where I might stumble on a bear or a mountain lion. Because of the place itself and my familiarity with it, I had a safe way to face some of my fears and learn to trust myself. I also had my cell phone and my dogs (sometimes a cat too!) with me.

In my experiment with walking in the woods in the dark, I knew I was safe in trying what I tried. If you do decide to do things to help with your fear, please be smart about it! Otherwise you may end up reinforcing your fear.

As you start facing your fears, you will begin to be able to tell the difference between a true fear—that is, a fear that provides guidance—and a fear that your mind is creating. As you get to know this difference, you will sense whether a threat is real or something created in your mind. For example, when that alleyway is just ahead and you ask yourself if the fear you feel about walking by it comes from an actual threat or from something your mind is creating, you'll be pretty sure of your answer.

Each year, as I start my walks in the dark again, different levels of fear come up. Each year it gets easier and easier to quiet the crazy fears and to open more fully to the guidance, trust, and flow. But each year, my mind still creates some fears and I am reminded of the cycle of life. Throughout the course of life, we will have fears arise that are created by our mind, but as we face and feel them more often, it gets easier and easier to dispel this type of fear. By facing fears, I have gotten more in touch with trust and guidance, and this has greatly enhanced my growth and trust in myself. I can feel as my mind tries to create fear and doubt, and I can connect into the flow.

As you play with this yourself and face your "monsters," you will be able to trust your true guidance more and more. As with each emotion, the key to connecting to your true guidance system is by letting yourself feel your way through the lies to the truth. Doing this, you can be more present. My mind was controlling me with visions from movies and scary stories from the past and it was going to keep me from enjoying myself in the woods. Since I was able to feel my reactions and then clear them, I was able to return to the present.

It's the same with all fears. They can be extremely paralyzing and keep you from growing. "What will my friends, family, partner think?" "What if I am judged?" "What if I get into trouble or get ostracized?"

These fears can be very powerful. To start to face them, you can ask yourself, "What is the worst that could happen?" In some cases, being true to yourself could cost you a relationship or even your life.

Sometimes the fear of being true to yourself could be rooted in an actual threat to your personal health. It takes a very courageous person to risk his safety to follow his true heart in such situations. People with this kind of courage have caused changes throughout history and doing so has cost many his or her life. One thing I know for sure: there comes a point in every life when we risk death with our decision. Being true to yourself might lead to harm of your physical body or death of your ego. However, if we aren't true to ourselves, it will definitely lead to harm or death of our spirit.

*Some possible benefits of fear:* Fear and its variants—panic, anxiety, terror, nervousness—can help keep you safe. Fear can guide you to slow down, or to stop, and to re-evaluate your current path. It is a warning that can protect you.

*Some possible limitations or pitfalls of fear:* Fear can keep you from trying new things and from following your true path. It can lead to being frozen, to fatigue and exhaustion, and to systemic disorders.

### Exercise: Uncovering Beliefs and Feelings about Fear and Its Variants

You can only learn to know the difference between the two kinds of fear by taking the time to clear your false fears. You clear the false fears by going into and feeling the fears that control you, asking, "Am I afraid of a real threat or of something my mind has created?" Clearing false fears will allow you to access the true guidance of fear, which is to help keep you safe. One way to do this is to put yourself in a safe situation that brings up some of your fears. To paraphrase a quote I love from Eleanor Roosevelt: Do something each day that scares you. You need to face your fears to grow. If you are afraid to speak in front of others, take a speech class. If you are afraid of dogs, go to an animal shelter and interact with the dogs (with guidance). I am not suggesting you act recklessly. This is about really looking at things that scare you and keep you from being real. Start with things that aren't particularly scary and work your way up. As you face and clear the fears controlling you, you can start taking back control of your life. Until then, you are controlled by your fears.

## Guilt, remorse, regret

Guilt appears in several forms, each revealing aspects of ourselves and our behaviors. In any given situation, you have to determine what it is that guilt is trying to show you. Guilt can point out behaviors you would like to change. You can approach feeling guilty as a cue to take time to pause and reflect, as an opportunity to see how you would like to change a way you acted that left you feeling guilty. Looking at your actions, you might decide you need to apologize or take steps to make sure you act differently the next time you are in that situation. This is a healthy form of guilt, one you learn to recognize, use appropriately, and release after it has served its purpose.

But this isn't always the case; it's not as simple as that. In many situations throughout our lives, we are taught to feel guilty when we act in a way others don't want us to act, even if we are acting according to our truth. The pitfall here is people using guilt as a way to control others. For example, you get passed a belief when you hear, "If you loved me, you would [or would *not*] say this or do that." Or, "I'm your mother so you need to do this for me." I call this the *obligation rule* and it teaches us to feel guilt as a trained response, not as guidance. When someone uses the obligation rule on you, you learn to feel guilty when that person gets upset because you didn't say or do the thing(s) you were "supposed to say" or "supposed to do" in a given situation, because you broke the obligation implied in the other person's statement. Submitting to these obligation rules is another way we change ourselves to try to please others or to receive conditional love from them. This form and use of guilt is unhealthy.

If you feel or hold onto guilt from breaking an obligation rule, you are just falling into a cycle of beating yourself up. If you find yourself using guilt to control others (and you will—it's what we have been programmed to do!), then notice it and start changing your behavior. As I keep saying about anything you feel, only by taking time to feel through it can you determine the nature of any guilt you may feel. Feeling through guilt, you can discover whether it is a pointer toward change and growth or a means by which you are letting others control and manipulate you (or by which you try to control or manipulate others).

Take stealing as an example. There are many forms of stealing, depending on how you look at things, and so all of us have probably stolen at some time or another. For instance, a small kid seeing if you can get away with it; taking supplies from your workplace; billing a customer for hours you didn't work… the examples are endless. Taking time to see how you justify your actions can be a great way to uncover beliefs and thoughts that are unhealthy for your soul. You might think, "Well, they don't pay me enough, so they owe me." Or, "They have so much money they'll never even miss it." Stealing usually comes from a fear of scarcity or from a feeling of entitlement.

If you steal, you may feel guilty or remorseful either because you were taught it is not appropriate to steal or because the action of stealing felt harmful to your spirit. This will give you an opportunity to feel through all the beliefs on stealing. You may think about the person you robbed and come up with many different beliefs that you feel either justify your actions or increase your guilt. If the person you robbed was rich and arrogant, you may feel justified, like Robin Hood. If the person you robbed was elderly, barely making it, and an overall nice human being, you may feel even more guilt.

Approach your sense of guilt with interest and see how you can talk yourself into and out of guilt using justification. To get to the bottom of the feelings that led you to the action in the first place, you will have to be compassionately honest as you weave your way through to the core. The action is usually just the symptom, not the problem. For instance, if you feel guilty about hitting a car and fleeing the scene, the underlying cause might be fear of getting into trouble or going to jail, each rooted in a fear of scarcity. Look at any of your guilty actions and then let your feelings take you to the beliefs, fears, and thoughts that led you to the action; let the guilt guide you to changing behaviors that go against your spirit. Guilt can prompt you to change how you act or to let go of the beliefs and thoughts which enable others to use guilt to control you.

We often use guilt in our relationships. Many of us have been taught to use guilt to manipulate others into staying in a relationship or as a way to prove to others how much we love them. For instance, "How can you do this to me?" Or, "You have to love me [or do this for me], because I did this, this, and this for you." That is conditional love, not unconditional love. The guilt is an attempt to keep someone small, weak. Using guilt to control and manipulate others is all about power, not love. To create a truly loving relationship, people must be willing to look at their guilt-driven beliefs and make the effort to transcend them.

Another example of how guilt can be used to keep someone small can be a family business. Suppose you want to be an artist, but your father makes wood furniture. You might join him in his business out of guilt, because he expected you to follow in his footsteps. You join him, but you are not being yourself. The guilt is keeping you from being true.

Sometimes you use guilt to keep yourself small. One way to tell if you are doing this is to ask yourself, "If my best friend had done this would I judge her for it?" Would you judge others as harshly as you're judging yourself? Most of us aren't nearly as hard on our friends as we are on ourselves. We are usually nicer to people—even those we don't like—than we are to ourselves! I like to remind myself of this fact: I am the only person I am going to be around for my life, so why not be someone whom I enjoy being around!

Every act happens for a reason. There are no mistakes, just opportunities to learn, heal, and grow. Many books discuss this concept in detail and offer a great way to really break free from the guilt that limits us and from the fear of making mistakes that can paralyze us. One such book is *Loving What Is,* by Byron Katie. Guilt isn't something that should be used by others to keep you small or used by you to keep others small. Guilt is a feeling that helps you know when you are doing something that is potentially damaging to your spirit or hindering your growth process. Someone once put it well, "The past is meant to be a guidepost, not a hitching post." If you keep yourself attached to that past situation because of guilt, anger, or the thought that it was wrong, you're not going to be able to move forward; you're just going to stay stuck in that spot. This is when forgiveness comes in; we'll get to that later in this book as we look at how growth involves a balance of stillness and movement.

*Some possible benefits of guilt, remorse, regret:* These feelings can lead you to change your behavior in a way that is healthier for your spirit. They can lead you to grow.

*Some possible limitations or pitfalls of guilt:* Guilt can be used to keep you small or to beat yourself up. It can be used for manipulation.

### Exercise: Uncovering Beliefs and Feelings about Guilt and Its Variants

If you feel guilty about something and decide you would like to act differently in the future, acknowledge and accept what you did, or said, or thought, and start taking the action necessary for a change to occur. Don't waste time by getting stuck in the guilt or in beating yourself up; that doesn't lead to growth. Action leads to growth. Feel through all the layers, beliefs, fears, and thoughts that lead you to the action and then ask yourself, "How would I like to act the next time I am in that situation?" This will lead you to act in a manner that follows your true path and is healthy for your soul.

### Joy, happiness, love

Now we look at the some of the emotions frequently labeled the "good" emotions: joy, happiness, and love. These emotions are often established as the "goal" of spiritual growth, the goal being a constant state of happiness and joy. So, why are so many people unhappy? Some of the unhappiness can come from trying to avoid the "negative" emotions and only wanting to feel the "positive" emotions. I hope the preceding examples have shown how feeling all emotions and letting go of value judgments about them can lead to tremendous growth and healing. This approach to emotions isn't merely beneficial; it is necessary and essential for growth and healing.

As I noted in the section on losing ourselves, almost everyone—no matter how great their life has been—has taken on the lies that they are not good enough or that they don't deserve love or joy. These beliefs can limit the ability to truly feel joy. Take some time and ask yourself, "Do I deserve to feel joy? Do I deserve to be happy?" Give yourself the time to sink deeply into these questions and see if you discover any beliefs you didn't even realize were there.

I discussed another topic in the section about losing ourselves that has bearing on our ability to feel joy and happiness. As you were growing up, you may have been told things like you were bad, you weren't good enough, or you were the black sheep of the family. Statements like these can become beliefs preventing you from feeling joy fully and being happy. This can lead you to doing things that sabotage yourself. These are the times when a good thing starts happening and you do something that reinforces the belief you are bad, or you don't deserve to be happy, or things have to be hard. As you take time to uncover these hidden stumbling blocks, you can start to not only bring more love and joy into your life but also experience the love and joy that have always been in your life!

If you believe you should always feel joyful and happy and come to find you aren't joyful or happy, you may conclude there's something wrong in your life. This usually leads to thinking something outside of you needs to change: "I am not happy, so I need to find something or someone to blame." This leads to the "if only" mindset that causes people to constantly change things around them in an attempt to finally "be happy." "If only I had more money." "If only my spouse would act how I want her (or him) to do." "If only I lived in the mountains."

"If only I had this job, or that person, in my life." The list is virtually endless. Unfortunately, this is the focus of many self-help or growth books: "If you just think positively and visualize what you want, then presto! You will get what you want and you will live happily ever after." This thinking sets people up for failure.

Keep in mind the principles of cycles and the spiritual truth "This too shall pass." Life is about motion and cycles. There are going to be times when you feel happy and joyous, others when you feel sorrow, and still others when you feel angry or guilty. And then, all of these times pass. You create problems when you try to figure out and label or justify all of these emotions as right or wrong or appropriate, instead of doing what you should with emotions: just feel them and use them as guidance. Use emotions to become more and more present and real. Feel when emotions are true guidance and when they are created by your mind. It's when you get stuck in the right or wrong and in trying to figure them out that you lose the guidance emotions can provide, and you become stagnant. Happiness and joy come when you truly realize each moment passes. If you're experiencing an emotion you are enjoying, enjoy it to the fullest knowing it will pass. If you're experiencing an emotion which is so difficult you can barely breathe, take comfort knowing it will pass; it will pass more quickly when you just feel it and let it go, instead of holding on or judging it.

*Some possible benefits of joy, happiness, love:* These feelings can lead to expansion, connection, healing, life!

*Some possible limitations or pitfalls of joy, happiness, love:* You may feel you don't deserve love, need to pretend to be happy when you're not (this builds more masks), or should always feel happy.

### Exercise: Uncovering Beliefs and Feelings about Joy and Its Variants

As you look into these "positive" emotions, you will once again need to uncover and observe the beliefs and thoughts that you have about them. You may have blockages of which you are not even aware, blockages that can be keeping you from having more happiness and joy in your life. Take some time to ask yourself the following questions. Give yourself time with each question and feel your responses to the question in your body, not just in your head. Let the initial responses come and go and see if there is anything under that layer of initial responses.

Ask yourself these questions:

- Is it okay to feel happy?

- Is it okay to feel good about myself?

- Is it okay to like myself?

- Do I deserve to feel joy?

The immediate response to each of these questions is usually, "Yes, of course I do!" But as you sit with the questions, some other thoughts may bubble up. We even have beliefs regulating when we should and shouldn't feel joy and when we do and don't deserve to feel love or to be loved. Uncovering these limiting beliefs and then changing them to healthier ones is an important part of healing, one often missed because we don't even know they are there. For instance, you might be unaware that you have a belief about whether it is okay for you to express joy when you are around someone who is grieving or depressed. As you start to uncover and become aware of these beliefs, you may be surprised at how much you temper your emotions based on who you are around and what their emotional state is at the moment.

In this section, I discussed how to start to communicate with the different sensations in your body. I also brought up how to listen without judgment and to feel down through the layers to the different beliefs that may be helping or hindering your growth. I also discussed how to connect in and feel where some of these beliefs may be stored in your body. Then I brought up some of the possible benefits and pitfalls of some of the emotions. All of this has been to suggest some different ways of looking at these emotions and various ideas about them.

Remember there can be countless reasons for every emotion and every sensation. It's important to stay away from trying to figuring out the "whys" and instead to just feel what is there. Take time to feel and embrace emotions and sensations. Become comfortable feeling. No one grows, or heals, or changes in their comfort zone. It often takes uncomfortable feelings to elicit change and growth and to allow our true and brilliant selves to shine through. All emotions and sensations have a purpose.

In the next section, I discuss how we can become more present again, doing so by consciously allowing the body to access layers in which beliefs, thoughts, and emotions might be stuck.

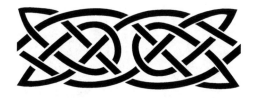

## Section 3

# Releasing Our True Self

In the first section of this book I discussed some of the ways we have lost the connection to our true self. In the second section I brought up some ideas on how to start to reconnect to the guidance system of your body, the physical and emotional sensations. The second section included a segment on using feeling to find those physical and emotional restrictions in the body which may be keeping you from restoring your physical function and from healing physically, and blocking you on your overall journey. Now that you have started to be able to connect to—to find and feel into—where these restricted places are in your body, the next step is learning how to help open up these physically restricted areas, which in turn will help lead to physical, emotional, and spiritual freedom.

Being able to help open up the physical aspect of your body is an important piece of the overall healing and growth process, a piece often overlooked. Many of us have been taught the wrong mentality to use in opening up the body in this way and so haven't been able to make the progress we would like to make. We need to be taught how important it is to release the actual physical restrictions in the body in order to progress toward physical, emotional, and even spiritual freedom. Physical restrictions often involve tissue memory, a form of memory found in each cell of your body. Tissue memory holds the sensations from past traumas, as well as the thoughts and beliefs about those traumas. Regardless of when the trauma occurred, the sensations, thoughts, and beliefs stored in tissue memory can be controlling every aspect of your life now.

In this section, I want to discuss further the importance of connecting to the felt sense in our healing process. I begin in the first chapter of this section (Chapter 11) by discussing some of the shortcomings in what both patients and healthcare professionals have been taught about the body. In Chapter 12, I discuss JFB-MFR. This is a form of bodywork that introduced me to the idea of applying universal principles to the body in a way that leads to working with the body to help achieve healing.

In Chapter 13, I describe the theory of tissue/cellular memory, the theory that cells can contain memory that affects you without your conscious awareness. I discuss how important it is to be able to release the restricted places in your body where these memories are stored, so you can free yourself from limitations that can stem from your past. In Chapter 14, I tie the universal principles of the body and of myofascial release to life principles. In Chapter 15, the final chapter of this section, I discuss the potential of freedom for your mind, body, and spirit.

## Chapter 11

## *Universal Principles and How They Apply to the Body*

Part of my knowledge of what is taught in healthcare comes from going through physical therapy school. The physical therapy students and the medical students took anatomy and dissection class together. So, what I was taught about anatomy was the same as what the physicians were taught. Most of what is taught to healthcare professionals is limited in that it fails to take into consideration universal principles as they apply to the body. Healthcare education also largely fails to consider how emotions, thoughts, and beliefs can have an effect on the body.

I also know about what is taught in healthcare from my experiences being a patient. I had problems with ovarian cysts and with back pain that led to multiple surgeries and then to chronic pain. Through my experiences in having these physical difficulties and working to resolve them, I learned what it is like to access the healthcare system—in both its traditional and alternative form—from the perspective of a person in pain trying to help her own body. This was a very frustrating time in my life, one in which I experienced firsthand the limitations of what is taught in traditional healthcare and often in holistic healthcare as well. It was also a time in my life that led me to a lot of wisdom and knowledge that I might not have gained if I hadn't had the surgeries and pain. My experience as a patient of the healthcare system made it very apparent to me that what we are taught in healthcare is very limited and does not follow universal principles.

When I use the term "universal principles" I am referring to ideas that are generally accepted when applied to various aspects of life. I will discuss this more at the end of this section. For now, I will state some of these universal principles which apply to the body and discuss how a particular universal principle applies to the body. I also describe the healthcare consequences of *not* applying that principle to the body.

### Everything is connected.

As it applies to the body, the universal principle that everything is connected means everything in the body is interconnected and each system in the body influences, and is influenced by, all the body's other systems and functions. In the body, *connective tissue*, called *fascia,* forms a three-dimensional network running through the entire body, from the top of your head to the tip of your toes. Every structure in the body—every nerve, blood vessel, muscle, tendon, ligament, organ, gland, bone, lymph vessel, and even every cell—is enmeshed in, interconnected by, and influenced by the fascia. This tissue has an effect on every system in your body.

In the anatomy classes I took in school, we were taught the subject matter in sections: the arm, the head, the hip, etc. We were taught the nervous system was responsible for this, the liver was responsible for that, the biceps caused this movement and resisted that one. We were taught the function of each muscle, nerve, artery, organ, and system as if it were an individual, separate, and unconnected entity.

Breaking a subject into sections is often necessary to teach the subject matter. However, the anatomy classes didn't bring the sections together as a whole at any point. In this book, I break the subject matter into different sections for the sake of discussion and then bring the sections together into a whole at the end. To help encourage you to see the subject of each section as part of a unified whole, I keep pointing out that life is dynamic and there is no set protocol for anything in it, that every aspect of your life is influenced by all the others, that all aspects of your life run together. In the anatomy classes in physical therapy school, the fact that everything is connected is missed. The different parts and systems of the body were taught in separate sections and they were not brought back together. We were not reminded that the body is a unified whole. What is missed is the universal principle that everything is connected.

An entire *system* of the body—the fascial system—was skipped when I was taught anatomy in physical therapy school. As I've said, every nerve, artery, muscle, and cell in your body is influenced by the fascia, and it is not discussed in detail in anatomy class. In dissection class, the only reference to the fascia was that it was the "stuff you need to clear out of the way so you can have access to the important parts of the body." We were not taught that trauma causes the fibers of this connective tissue to tighten, or to adhere to adjacent structures, or both. Nor were we taught that fascia can produce up to 2000 pounds of pressure per square inch (2000 psi). Think about that for a moment: the restrictions in the fascial system—that is, the places where the fascia has tightened—can be literally crushing the nerves, arteries, lymphatic vessels, muscles, organs, and cells in your body. Yet, most of the healthcare professionals were not taught about this possibility and its possible effects on the body.

To have hope of attaining a state of overall health and balance, we, and those from whom we receive healthcare, must apply to the body the universal principle that everything is connected.

**Every living organism is unique and dynamic.**

As it applies to the body, the universal principle that every living organism is unique and dynamic means no two bodies are exactly alike and every body is constantly changing. I am sure you have heard the statement that no two snowflakes are the same. This is true for the human body too. Even in the case of identical twins, there is a difference in the make-up of each twin's body because each twin's life is unique. Your own body's scars, restrictions, muscle development, and so forth are the result of what you have done in your life. Every body is different from every other body.

The education of healthcare professionals forgets the universal principle that every living organism is unique and dynamic. Healthcare professionals are taught to try to fit patients into certain categories (i.e., to make a diagnosis) based on the patients' symptoms. Unfortunately, this approach ignores the principle that every body is unique and dynamic.

For example, when five people with shoulder pain go to a physician, the physician is likely to use the symptom-diagnosis approach he or she learned in school. Each patient will likely be given tests, prescriptions, or referrals focused on the symptom's location—the shoulder—rather than on another location which may be causing the symptom. Since healthcare professionals are taught to segment and separate the body, and to focus on the symptoms, the tests may include X-rays, MRIs, muscle or joint tests, all focused on the shoulder. The physician will likely prescribe a care plan that is a protocol, one he or she learned to follow based on a symptom, or set of symptoms, and on a test result or group of results. As likely as all the rest of the details in this example, the single protocol applied to each of the five patients will affect each patient differently, each experiencing a degree of improvement somewhere between none at all and complete recovery.

The approach in the preceding example is by far the most common approach in healthcare. This approach forgets that everything is connected and then augments that mistake by failing to take into account that every body is different. Healthcare's omission of these two principles leads to so many people having unrelieved chronic pain, physical dysfunction, and systemic issues.

What if we applied this healthcare philosophy—segment the body; diagnose and treat based on symptoms—to situations outside of healthcare? If your car had a part that kept breaking and the mechanic kept replacing that part each time it broke, how long would you continue to go to that mechanic? If the same part kept breaking, you wouldn't allow the part to be replaced again and again; you would want to find out what was causing the part to break. You would sense that something was happening in the car that caused excessive strain or stress on the part, causing the part to break. Continuing to replace the part wouldn't fix the problem; that approach would be focusing on the symptom— the part that is breaking—rather than the problem—the source of the excessive stress.

Consider another example, one from construction. Suppose a structure became unstable or actually broke. The builder or engineer wouldn't just reinforce the unstable area or replace the part of the structure that broke; he would also determine the location of the excess stress that caused the instability or break in that area.

Unfortunately, healthcare typically focuses on the symptom rather than looking for its cause. Consider the typical treatment for an extremely common symptom: back pain. If someone has degenerating, bulging, or ruptured discs, stress is building in the back at the location of the symptoms and the breakdowns, but the source of the stress is usually located elsewhere. This is why so many back surgeries fail both in reducing or alleviating pain and in increasing or restoring mobility. Doctors are taught to reinforce the weak spot by fusing the symptom area, the area affected by the stress. They are not taught to find the source of the stress and then alleviate the cause of the problem.

After such a back surgery, the patient will more than likely be sent to a therapist who was also taught the same thing, to focus on and treat the symptom. The therapist will focus on strengthening the core muscles to help support the place under stress, the place where the symptoms are located. Rarely does the therapist expand the treatment to include finding and treating the place from which the stress comes, which would help prevent the injury occurring again. This is why most people continue to have back problems after spinal fusion; they injure the back in the same place, or, the force now causes problems above or below the fusion, since the cause of the problem wasn't addressed. Referring to the preceding construction example, the same kind of problem would occur if the builder continued to reinforce the point where the structure continued to break, instead of locating the cause of the stress: the structure would keep collapsing.

Let's consider the example of the back injury in light of how the fascial system might be involved and how its involvement might be missed by a healthcare practitioner. A number of important characteristics of the fascial system are relevant here. To review, the fascial system is made up of connective tissue that connects the entire body in a three-dimensional network from head to toe; it can affect every part of the body. It is rarely, if ever, discussed in healthcare education, and so healthcare providers rarely, if ever, consider it in their evaluation and diagnosis of physical conditions. When fascial tissue is traumatized, it can form restrictions (areas of tightness) that can exert up to 2000 psi, a force capable of literally crushing delicate structures such as nerves and blood vessels. Add to these characteristics the fact that fascial restrictions do not show up on any existing diagnostic tests—not X-rays, MRIs, CAT scans, blood work, or *any* other diagnostic tests. Consequently, healthcare practitioners do not take these restrictions into account when a patient has physical pain or systemic issues.

In the preceding back pain example, the symptom is back pain, usually caused by the breakdown of tissue or of other structures such as muscles or discs. This kind of breakdown can also put pressure on nerves. The symptom is the back pain, but what is the cause? Where is the pressure coming from that is causing the breakdown of the tissue? If the focus is only on the symptom, then the body will never return to balance and health. The force can be coming from anywhere in the body.

A typical pattern I have found is that there is often a fascial restriction in the *front* of the body due to some form of trauma—accident, surgery, child birth, repetitive stress from postural positions involved in work, etc.. As a result of the trauma, the fascia tightens down in the front, pulling the body forward with a force that can exert up to 2000 pounds of pressure per square inch. To get an understanding of this force, it would be similar to walking around all day holding a cement block out in front of you. The sensation of this pulling forward may feel like holding a cement block out in front all day long. Consequently, the muscles in the back of the body must contract continuously to keep the body in an upright position. The restricted tissue is literally cemented down, so the effects of the stress do not always show up in the front; instead, the stress affects the muscles, joints, discs, and ligaments on the back side of the body, as these are the structures which work constantly to counteract the pulling force originating from the fascial restriction on the front. Restrictions in the front of the body are the main cause for neck, upper back, and lower back problems, yet they are rarely, if ever, addressed.

Actually, the body often does show stress where the restrictions are located, but they are usually symptoms that aren't generally associated with a tissue problem, so they usually get treated with medications. Some of the symptoms that can be caused by restrictions in the front of the body (the abdomen) are irritable bowel syndrome, fertility issues, menstruation issues, acid reflux, and asthma. Many of these symptoms can be affected by fascial restrictions.

Treating the problem's symptoms instead of finding the problem's origin is one of the downfalls of the healthcare system. Another downfall is once a person is diagnosed, treatment is typically a protocol dictated by the symptoms and the diagnosis. This protocol-based approach to treatment fails to take into account the dynamic individual. Instead, it treats people as if they were all the same, regardless of shape, size, sex, nationality, or life experience.

Let's apply this type of thinking to the preceding example from the construction industry. It would be like saying that the same kind of foundation for a house could be used in the mountains of Oregon, on the sandy banks of North Carolina, and on the desert rock in Arizona. It's not hard to see that using the same materials and design for a foundation on each of these different surfaces and different climates wouldn't work well. Why don't we see that obvious fact about treatment for people in the healthcare field? The only way to help someone truly achieve health is to remember that each person is dynamic and unique.

### Meet at the barrier. If you force, you get resistance.

If the body perceives something as forceful, it will resist that force. Meeting at the barrier means connecting with the body in a way that is not perceived as forceful, which will then allow the body to release and heal instead of brace and guard.

This is the same when applied outside of the body too. For example, if you place your hand softly on top of water, it sinks into the water. But, if you slap the water, the water resists your hand. The same is true with kneading dough. If you let your hands sink in and knead with firm but not forceful pressure, you can form the dough easily into the shape you want. But if you knead with too much force, the dough will crack and resist your hands. This is also true with the body.

In physical therapy school, some of the techniques I was taught were forceful. We weren't taught how to listen to the body and to let it guide us. You may have heard the saying "No pain, no gain." It isn't true. I have heard physical therapists referred to as "physical terrorists." Some therapists actually take that as a compliment!

In school, I never did quite understand the philosophy of forcing a knee to bend after a total knee replacement. I had undergone a knee surgery in high school and afterward needed to have my knee immobilized for a month. Needless to say, my knee was very stiff after the immobilizer was removed. At the time, I lived in a rural community and did not have access to physical therapists or athletic trainers. (Knowing what I know now, I have to say I was probably lucky I didn't have access to these professionals. They might have used forceful stretches on me, the same forceful stretches I would learn later in physical therapy school for use on patients with a stiff knee.) I learned that if I applied a gentle tension over a period of time, my knee would slowly give. It took time, but it released and was not painful.

When we were taught in physical therapy school to force the knee to start bending right after surgery, it didn't make practical sense to me because I knew there was a less painful and more productive way to help the knee regain mobility. It didn't make sense to force the knee to bend, causing the person unnecessary pain. I knew that if I did so, then the next time I walked in the room, the patient would start bracing in anticipation of more pain, already setting up for a battle.

Force leads to resistance. We shouldn't have to battle the body, we should be taught how to work with the body and give it time to release. Just like the example with the dough, we should learn how to apply just enough pressure to help reform the tissue in the body to its true elastic state, instead of forcing it and potentially causing damage. Our body is amazing. It knows how to digest food, how to release chemicals needed to keep itself in harmony, how to repair damaged cells, and so on. Our body knows what it needs. If you add only enough pressure to engage restricted tissue (which means not using so much pressure that you attempt to force the restricted tissue to stretch) and give it time, it will release in a gentle way that will break up the restrictions without damaging healthy tissue. It is very easy to feel the difference between pressure that engages and then releases a restriction, and pressure that attempts to force the restriction. If you are using pressure that releases a restriction, the process may be painful, but the tissue will soften and give. If you are forcing and potentially damaging healthy tissue, then the muscles will actively resist the force by contracting and guarding.

Unfortunately, most therapists were not taught this approach. Instead, most were taught to go as deep and hard as the patient could tolerate. Sometimes we were even taught to use tools to help us dig deeper into the tissue, a method that can actually cause damage to healthy tissue. Breaking up the tissue in a forceful way may lead to short term improvements in mobility, but in 3 to 6 months or so, the healthy tissue that was damaged will tighten. The result is often that the patient ends up being even more restricted and bound down than was the case before treatment. Being aware of the universal principle that force provokes resistance, and engaging restrictions without attempting to force through them, will help prevent unnecessary pain and damage to the body.

**Change takes time.**

For long lasting changes to take place in the body, it takes time. As I noted before, if a system is forced, it will resist, be damaged, or break. This is also true with rushing or not allowing enough time. Moving too quickly can have the same effect as forcing, causing damage or producing only temporary changes. When you engage the system without forcing, and give it enough time, the tissue can start to rearrange and release. Tissue that has been damaged and has become restricted or scarred down can have some or all of its elasticity restored if it's given enough time.

Research has shown it takes a minimum of 90-120 seconds of maintaining tension at the barrier of the tissue to even start to elicit a long lasting change in the tissue. Stop and think about that for a moment. That means the change *starts* to occur at 1½ minutes. It is recommended to hold the tension in stretched tissue for a minimum of *3-5 minutes* to get a good release. This is why a lifetime of 15-30 second stretches never produces a significant release. Stretching 15-30 seconds may cause the tissue to lengthen for a few minutes or a day, but it never lasts. I stretched for sports from middle school through college and never had anything but a temporary change in my muscles and now I know why. Usually the stretch was too forceful, going into end range instead of just engaging at the barrier, and it was not held long enough.

One of the thoughts on how this tissue change occurs is the *piezoelectric effect*. In very simple terms, the piezoelectric effect is a phenomenon that causes a structure to change when a low-level force is applied to the structure over time. When tissue is engaged using just enough tension—through either elongation or direct pressure—and that tension is held for a specific amount of time, the tissue can start to regain some of its elasticity. For the tissue in our body, this time is 1½ minutes for the tissue to *start* to change; it is recommended to hold for a minimum of 3-5 minutes.

This method of treating tissue can start to release some of the restrictions that were putting up to 2000 psi of pressure on various structures in the body. This approach allows the tissue to move more easily and can decrease pressure on and damage to joints, ligaments, muscles, arteries, organs, and all forms of tissue, down to the cellular level. As we make these simple changes in how we treat the body, it will result in significant improvements. By eliminating force and adding more time, we can help the body to return to health. I will give practical examples that tie these principles together in Chapter 15.

### There is a flow to life.

Life has a flow. To apply this principle to the body, you need to connect with your body and allow yourself to be guided. Most forms of therapy teach protocols for treating symptoms and this is why so many people struggle with chronic pain. As you learn to connect into your body through self-treatment and through movement exercises, you can find the location of your restrictions or barriers and start to free yourself. To do this, you want to follow the path of least resistance and go with the flow.

In treatment, this means that as the tissue releases, you want to follow the release, or take the slack out of the tissue, so you can maintain the pressure at the barrier. This is what allows the release to go deeper and deeper into the tissue. Consider this concept in terms of the preceding dough example. As your hand rests on the dough, you will eventually feel your hand sinking into the dough. If you maintain the pressure without forcing, your hand will continue to sink more and more over time. The same thing occurs with the tissue.

## Life has cycles.

You need to apply the universal principle that life has cycles to your body and to your healing process. Neither your growth nor your body's healing will be linear. There will be days when you feel an ease and grace with your movement, and there will be days when you feel locked down and tight. Many people are taught the body will become progressively tighter as we age, but that doesn't have to be the case. When you learn how to listen to your body and how to help it release, you can keep your body as flexible and as healthy as possible. Your body is dynamic and has cycles just like everything else. Don't expect your body to be linear with its progress or its decline. Don't fall into the trap of feeling there will be an end point. The cycles will continue throughout your entire life.

## Truths are a felt sense.

It takes feeling to know your truths and to know what is happening. No matter how much you think about an activity, you can't predict what will happen in life; there are too many variables. You have to stop thinking and get into the action. In this case, that means feeling. You need to use your sensations—the physical and emotional sensations and all the guidance of your spirit—to guide you along your process. You need to connect to yourself and to the entire universe if you want to become fully empowered. Touch is something sorely missing in current healthcare. Diagnostics are done by machines. Most doctors already have an idea of a diagnosis before they even look at, talk to, or touch a patient. They collect the data from the tests and already have a decision formulated before they even enter the room. This is the same with most therapists. Again, the problem is these practitioners are primarily looking at and treating symptoms. It takes connecting with and feeling the body to get true information.

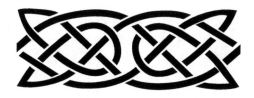

# Chapter 12

## John F. Barnes' Myofascial Release: Bodywork Incorporating Universal Principles

### What is John F. Barnes' Myofascial Release?

The following is a very quick and limited explanation of John F. Barnes' Myofascial Release (JFB-MFR). To get a more thorough understanding of JFB-MFR, please refer to the many articles and books written by John F. Barnes, PT. You can also look at his website, www. myofascialrelease.com. The website describes the scientific rationale behind his approach and an extensive list of references. This will give you a basic understanding of the technique.

True JFB-MFR is a full-body, hands-on technique, developed and refined by John F. Barnes. This technique releases the fascial system, a three-dimensional web that connects and surrounds every system and cell in the body. I like to compare the human body to an orange to help people get the idea of the role of the fascial system. The thick, white, hard tissue that holds the peel onto an orange is similar to the fascia that holds the skin onto the body. When you cut an orange in half, you see the white fibers that separate the orange into chambers. Fascia in the body helps to separate the organs, muscles, and sections; it also keeps everything in place. Without the divisions created by the fascia, everything inside the body would shift with us when we stand up or move. When you look at an individual orange slice, you see the white fibers weaving throughout the slice, holding the slice together and also holding in the juice. This is very similar to the fascial system holding our bodies together down to the cellular level. Our bodies are over 70% fluid and the fascial system is what keeps all this fluid in the right places.

Through trauma and repetitive motion or positioning (e.g., lifting all day or sitting all day) restrictions can form in the fascial system. These restrictions can have the force of 2000 psi. This force can then literally crush any of the structures around it. Since the fascial system runs throughout your entire body, these restrictions can cause pain anywhere in the body and compromise every system. By system I mean vascular, neurological, muscular, circulatory, digestive, etc. This means fascial restrictions can cause digestive, fertility, circulation, neurological, and muscular problems, and can reproduce any symptom throughout the body. These restrictions can become tighter over time, literally making you feel like you are in a straightjacket.

JFB-MFR is a form of bodywork that follows the universal principles and can help remove the straitjacket from your body. A skilled therapist looks at and treats the entire body, helping to restore balance. Releasing the fascial restrictions throughout the body decreases the crushing force of fascial restrictions, which in turn increases function, decreases pain, increases blood flow and nutrition to the body, and increases overall health down to the cellular level.

By developing sensitivity through taking courses and being treated, a skilled JFB-MFR therapist can see and feel these fascial restrictions. After locating a restriction, the therapist engages the barrier of the restriction and allows the restriction to release. The barrier is the point at which the fascial restriction is in a lengthened position. This barrier occurs at a point *before* the end range of motion. Once the restriction is lengthened, it needs to be held for a minimum of 90-120 seconds before it *starts* to release. For a good release to occur, the restriction needs to be held at the barrier at least 3-5 minutes. If the therapist does not engage the barrier and wait 3-5 minutes for release, then he is not doing authentic JFB-MFR, not allowing the tissue to make a permanent change, and providing only temporary relief.

True JFB-MFR is not forceful. The body is allowed to release, not forced to release. This does not mean the releases will not be painful. Many times during a release, pain and many other sensations may be felt. This is described more completely in the following chapters.

It is essential that the therapist who treats you follow these guidelines:

1.  looks at and treats your entire body;
2.  engages the barrier and does not force though the barrier;
3.  holds at the barrier for at least 3-5 minutes to allow for a true release to occur;
4.  does not force or lead you; and
5.  does not interpret what you are feeling. Each person's experience is unique.

As I stated before, these are universal principles being applied to the body. If your therapist is not following these guidelines, she may not fully understand the principles of JFB-MFR. Many therapists take one or two classes from John, or take a class in school, and then advertise that they are doing MFR, but they don't really get the key factors. It's okay to question your therapist. If you have concerns, remember you can always voice them on the MFR chat line, found at www.myofascialrelease.com. This is a nice support system and a really good way to have your questions answered and your concerns addressed.

## How is JFB-MFR different from other forms of therapy?

The main difference between JFB-MFR and other forms of bodywork is how the universal principles are involved. Most forms of therapy and bodywork do not follow the principles that everything is connected and that every body is different. Instead, they generally follow protocols, using "cookbook techniques." As I stated earlier, most therapists and doctors have been taught to treat the symptom, segment the body, segment the emotional and physical sensations, and ignore the power of the consciousness.

JFB-MFR is a whole body technique that engages the fascia; understands the importance of emotions, thoughts, and beliefs in the healing process; and follows what the body needs instead of following protocols. JFB-MFR therapists are taught to connect with the body at the barrier, wait for the release, and then follow the release. In his seminars, John teaches therapists, "If you know what you are doing before you walk in the room, then you don't know what you are doing." He teaches that every time a therapist interacts with a client, he should treat the interaction as a new experience. If the therapist has preconceived ideas about what should be treated, he will not be able to remain objective during the treatment. Each session, the therapist should see where the body is restricted at that time and treat accordingly.

Most of the other forms of bodywork do not hold the barrier for 3-5 minutes, failing to allow for the fascia to change and thus producing only temporary changes in the body and its symptoms. The collagenous aspect of the fascial complex is what allows the tissue to regain length and it takes time for this collagenous aspect to release. It also takes time for the tissue to open and release what is called "tissue memory;" when this happens, emotions and beliefs can surface, be expressed, and be released. When you release tissue memory, you can truly heal issues. I will discuss this more in the chapter on tissue memory.

The awareness cultivated and used by JFB-MFR therapists is another big difference between JFB-MFR and other types of bodywork and traditional therapies. Awareness is needed to feel the restrictions and to be able to hold at the barrier. This barrier changes during the treatment as the fascia starts to release. The therapist needs to stay focused and centered to be able to feel the changes in the barrier, keeping at the barrier to keep the system engaged. If too much force is applied, the body starts to resist. If not enough force is applied, change occurs only in the elastic component, producing only temporary results. It takes a therapist who is aware and centered to be able to maintain the barrier as the fascia releases. This is why it's important that the therapist who treats you has been taught at a John Barnes seminar: this awareness and feel cannot be learned through a book. This is also why some therapists are better than others. A therapist may have gone to John's courses, but if he is not able to stay centered it will be more difficult or even impossible for him to feel the subtle changes that occur during a release.

True JFB-MFR does not injure, results in permanent changes, and can help a person heal in mind, body, and spirit. The reason JFB-MFR is non-injurious is due to the therapist's awareness during a treatment, to the ability to feel and not force the barrier. This is also what allows the full healing capability of the body to occur. The reason JFB-MFR can help a person heal in mind and spirit is because the consciousness is recognized and enhanced. JFB-MFR is about helping to empower the client by teaching her how to connect with and communicate with her body and how to treat herself. John teaches that without awareness, there is no choice. He encourages therapists to help their clients, and themselves, become aware that thoughts, beliefs, attitudes, and emotions can all have an impact on the healing process. All of these aspects together are why JFB-MFR is called authentic healing.

Chapter 13

*Tissue Memory and Its Effect on Healing*

Recent research has proven what John F. Barnes has been teaching for over 40 years: memories are stored in the cells of the body. This phenomenon is variously referred to as muscle memory, tissue memory, or cellular memory. Most people easily understand an example of what is called muscle memory as it applies to sports. If we didn't have muscle memory, athletes would have to relearn how to shoot a basket, hit a baseball, or throw a football each time they played a game. Muscles have memories and, with practice, the actions they perform can be done without thought.

A common experience associated with having the stomach flu provides a ready example of tissue or cellular memory. If you have gotten sick with the stomach flu, what happened the next time you smelled or tasted the food you ate before you got sick? Typically, you will have some sort of physical response to that smell or taste. Your stomach might get queasy, you might start to sweat, and you might even come close to throwing up. Your body is reacting to a memory. Your body associates the smell or taste of that food with becoming sick, and your body doesn't want to be sick again! So, when you smell or taste that food again, your body reacts with a physical response. That reaction reminds you of how sick you were previously and thereby tries to prevent you from causing the same thing to happen again. And even though you try to tell your body it's okay to eat this food, and you aren't sick, you can't make the sensation stop. When tissue memory is triggered, it takes over, and logical thought can't stop it.

When this kind of physical response occurs, your body is responding to a proprioceptive trigger. Proprioception involves sight, smell, taste, hearing, and touch. When receptors for any of these senses are triggered, tissue memory can occur, as in the preceding example. Another common tissue memory is stimulated by a sound proprioceptor: having a memory associated with a song. You hear a certain song and you are "taken back" to a significant time in your life. The song might be one from a wedding, a funeral, or a prom. Not only do you remember the event, but you may also feel emotions that surrounded the event.

Tissue memory can also be triggered when the fascia is released through touch (one of the proprioceptors). If an area being released was injured during a frightening event—a car accident, a fall, abuse, etc.—sensations that occurred during the event may also be released. You might feel fear, your body might shake, you might feel the pain just as intensely as when the trauma actually occurred. In short, you might feel any or all of the sensations caused during the trauma and since then trapped in the fascia and in your body.

As an example of tissue memory, consider what happens to someone in a car accident. Suppose a man is in a car that gets broadsided at an intersection by a car that didn't stop at a stop sign. Any time after he has that experience, the man may tense up and brace whenever he drives through an intersection and sees another car approaching the stop sign, even though the other car is obviously stopping at the stop sign. When tissue memory is triggered, it "takes over." You are unable to make it stop. When you have an incident happen that triggers tissue memory, you are actually becoming aware of what your body is feeling all the time on the subconscious level. What you need to do now is feel these sensations fully so they can be released from your body.

Feeling these sensations associated with tissue memory *fully* is easy to say, but not necessarily easy to do. When tissue memory occurs, the sensations can feel as intense as they did during the initial trauma itself. The sensations that occur in trauma are often overwhelming, which is why we often don't release those sensations in the first place. We leave the body when we are overwhelmed by pain, fear, etc.; this is one of our automatic self-defense mechanisms. By "leave the body," I mean we can become completely numb and block off the memory of the pain and emotions.

When the tissue is opened up and the sensations, beliefs, and thoughts are released, the experience can feel just as overwhelming as did the original trauma. The difference is that this time you are in control of the situation; you don't have to feel it all at once. You can chip away at it bit by bit. This is another reason it is important to receive treatments by a skilled therapist, one trained by John F. Barnes, who can help you with your process. When tissue memory surfaces, it's important to remind yourself that you are now safe and that the traumatic event is over. Then you can take the opportunity to feel the tissue memory and release it so you can live fully in the present. You can realize it's time to let yourself heal.

Opening up the tissue—by following the principles of meeting at the barrier and waiting—allows you access to the core of your limiting beliefs and to when and how you took on those beliefs. Opening up the tissue will also open up and allow you to release tissue memory, that is, any emotions or sensations that may have been trapped in your tissue and preventing you from healing fully. Once these emotions, sensations, and beliefs are brought up from the subconscious to the conscious level, you can actively choose to change or release them. However, until you release the container that has trapped these sensations and beliefs, you will be spinning and fighting the same battles again and again. You will continue to be driven by your subconscious, the part of the mind that is acting as if the trauma is still occurring. To your tissues, you still may be bracing for the impact or fighting for your life.

No matter how much you repeat the affirmation "I love myself," if you have the belief in your tissue that you are a bad person, you will not truly believe that affirmation. How might this belief get trapped in your body? Here are a couple of examples. If you are emotionally abused, your body tightens down just as it would if you were to receive physical blows. As your body tightens in response to the abuse, the emotions and beliefs you feel at the time can be trapped in the tissue. If you are in a car accident, you might experience physical and emotional sensations, and be aware of beliefs, that come up during the trauma; any of these can get trapped in your body. Long after the trauma is passed, you may have fear, anger, or other emotions trapped in your body. The belief "I could die" might flash through you during the accident; a part of you may not be able to stop bracing, even after your tissue has healed, because of the belief that if you stop bracing, you may die.

The beliefs and emotions held in tissue memory can be very powerful and cannot be "thought away." They can only be addressed when the tissue is released using a technique like JFB-MFR. Only by engaging the barrier and allowing the time needed for the barrier to release will you be able to access these emotions, sensations, and beliefs and allow yourself to heal truly.

Chapter 14

*Applying the Universal Principles to Life*

To help you on your path of growth, you can and should apply these universal principles to all aspects of your life—physical, emotional, and spiritual. As you continue to expand your knowledge, you will see these principles can be found in all the spiritual practices and in all the religions.

### Examples of the universal principles as applied to our physical surroundings

John F. Barnes describes various ways of pulling a blade of grass out of the ground to illustrate the universal principles of meeting at the barrier, applying just enough force for tension, and allowing. Pinch a blade of grass between your fingers and pull upward. You'll find if you apply too much pressure by pulling too hard (forcing the barrier), you snap the blade of grass. But if you apply just enough tension and then hold long enough (thus allowing the changes to occur), you reach a point where you feel the blade giving and the entire blade of grass will come out of the ground, roots and all (the release). The same is true of pulling roots or weeds out of the ground. Try it sometime!

Another example of these same principles was demonstrated to me on a hiking trip. I was among a group of myofascial release therapists who had gone hiking, leaving our cars parked in an area that had a time limit. When we got back to our cars after our hike, big florescent stickers on the driver's side windows informed us that we had parked there too long. Most of us started scraping away at the stickers, grumbling as we shredded the stickers bit by bit. While we labored away at this, my friend and fellow therapist called out to us, "Hey guys, haven't you heard of a thing called myofascial release? Just take a little of the sticker, apply just the right tension and wait [she was demonstrating as she spoke] and eventually... Presto!" And it was true. If you force a sticker by pulling too hard or getting impatient and not waiting, the sticker will rip. But if you apply just enough tension and wait, the adhesive will give over time and the sticker will come off in one piece.

On one occasion, I was explaining to a client of mine the reasoning behind the principles of myofascial release. This client is a mechanic and he understood what I meant very quickly. He explained that he uses the same principles when removing rusted bolts. He learned that if he applied just enough pressure to cause tension—but not so much as to force and break the bolt—and waited long enough, the bolt would give way eventually and remove easily. He went on to say that most of his coworkers couldn't understand his method and instead would get impatient, apply too much force, and end up breaking off the bolts.

### Examples of applying these principles to relationships

*Meet at the barrier.* If you force, you'll get resistance. This is a principle of life. Anything you force, whether it's a physical force or a person, will resist. If you try to force someone to understand your point of view or to believe what you believe, you'll get resistance. If you can meet the person at their emotional and cognitive levels, the two of you can work together and make progress. But any time you force, you're going to get resistance. It's the same thing with war or any other kind of conflict. If you can let go of force and find some common ground from which to work, you can make progress. It's a question of finding balance between speaking what is true to your spirit, surrendering, melding, meeting, and joining. Forcing comes from the ego and leads to resistance and conflict. As part of all this, you also need to be open to being dynamic; there is never just one way.

*Wait and allow.* You need to give things time to change. This is especially hard for those living in the USA, where people are programmed to expect and even demand instant results. Time is needed for things to process, for all the necessary factors to line up to bring about a change. If you try to rush things, you will find the process is very difficult or stops repeatedly.

## Examples of applying these principles to our journey

Most of this book is about applying the universal principles to your journey. Your journey is all about finding a balance, enhancing your connection, allowing time, adding feeling to your healing, realizing there will be cycles of ups and downs, going with the flow, and celebrating your uniqueness and dynamism. As you read on, you will find many examples of how to connect, meet at the barrier, and give time to feel your way through to healing.

## Examples of applying these principles to our bodies

You can take any stretch or exercise you do and change it by adding the universal principles to it. Add the principle of meeting your body: if you force, you will cause bracing and possibly injure yourself. Pay attention to what you do as you exercise or treat yourself: is your self-treatment or exercise a healthy practice or is it something potentially harmful? Add the time component: you need to give your body the time to release. Remember that it takes at *minimum* of 1½ minutes for the tissue to *start* to change; a good guideline for effective release is to hold it at the barrier for a minimum of 3-5 minutes. As you are self-treating, feel the connection in your body. Let go of treating symptoms and open up to feeling for the location of the cause.

These are just some examples of these universal principles and how they can be applied to all aspects of life—to our physical surroundings, our relationships, our bodies, and our journey of growth. These principles have been used in different forms of bodywork since the beginning of mankind. Exceptional teachers like John F. Barnes have been able to recognize the need to apply these principles in the healing process. He encourages his students to apply these principles to every aspect of their lives in order to truly live a healthy and empowered life.

If you want to change something in your life, if you have a conflict in your life, if you are trying to get goals in your life, remember: meet at the barrier and wait, allow things to happen, and then a flow will occur. As soon as you start to push too hard, tension will occur or things will break. If you start forcing, life will return your force in the same proportion you apply it. As you practice using these principles more and more, you will start to be able to feel when you are going with the flow of life and when you are forcing. This will lead you toward true freedom.

## Chapter 15

*Freedom*

What is freedom? Freedom is the release from the bonds, tethers, beliefs, and restrictions that keep you from becoming and retaining your true self. When bodywork follows the life principles, as does JFB-MFR, you can start to release these restrictions and remove the straitjacket that has been binding you and has been limiting your healing and growth. You can become more aware of your subconscious holding patterns, and of the beliefs and the lies your false self accepts, all of which have been keeping you from healing and from moving forward. Beliefs like "I'm not good enough" or "I deserve to be hurt" and lies like "If you are good, you will be rewarded" or "Only bad people have pain or discomfort" lead to subconscious holding or bracing patterns. These subconscious bracing patterns can literally lock your body and can crush its tissues, structures, and cells, leading to physical pain and dysfunction.

As I stated earlier, the fascial system runs through your entire body three-dimensionally, so restrictions can simulate any kind of physical symptom and can also cause systemic problems. Through receiving treatment by a therapist trained in the techniques I've been describing, and also by learning to treat yourself, you can start down a path of freedom. Not only will you help to free the physical body so it can perform the way it's supposed to do, but you can also have the opportunity to free yourself from limiting beliefs and lies, thereby enabling your emotional and spiritual growth.

As you release restrictions and become aware of the beliefs and the life patterns limiting your growth, you can then make the conscious choices. You can consciously choose to change your actions and to let go of limiting beliefs, thereby enhancing your growth and healing. You can also consciously choose to repeat your previous actions and to hold on to your limiting beliefs, thereby keeping you from growing or healing.

This is what I will go into in the next section—awareness and choice. When you have a lie—one like "I'm not good enough"—come to the surface, that's the time when you have a real and powerful choice available. Are you going to continue to believe the lie or are you going to step into the truth? It seems like an easy choice to make, but it is not always easy to do. Starting to become your true self, starting to change, affects everyone around you too. Once you become surer of yourself and start to value yourself more, you may not be the person you used to be. You won't be controlled or manipulated as easily as you used to be and you won't believe all the lies. Often, those around you were very comfortable with the person you used to be; some people will not want you to grow and heal.

So, it might seem easy to grow and heal, but a common theme in spiritual writings is that to become your true self fully, and to grow and heal, you have to be willing to lose everything you know. Everything you know and hold as true was built on a foundation that also included lies and false beliefs. You will need to go through a dismantling of everything you thought was true so you can actually step into your real truth. You have to be willing to "lose it all" to gain it all. This can be very scary to you and to those around you.

With bodywork like JFB-MFR, you can release tissue memory. Releasing tissue memory can help you get to the core of your symptoms and also to unlock the limiting beliefs and emotions preventing you from healing. When you get to the core, then it's up to you to choose whether you will step into healing or not. No one can make that final step but you. No one can heal you, healing is an active, participatory process.

Now that you know how to get to the places with restrictions and tissue memory, and how to release them, the next step is about your awareness, your choices; it's about returning to your true self. How do you do that? There are millions of different paths and every path is unique. In the next few chapters, I give you some ideas that have helped me along my journey. These ideas are stepping stones you can use to start to heal and to choose to step into your own greatness. Use whatever combinations work for you and branch out from them. I'm sure you'll also find other ways that will help you in your growth.

But, until you release your restrictions at the core level, you will not be able to move forward. You will keep fighting the same symptoms. John F. Barnes likes to say that changes that don't get to the core are like shoveling fog. You can shovel all you want—you can try to change everything you want by thinking or being in your head—but you just get tired and nothing really changes. Until you tap into your core, the place where you hold your limiting beliefs, and release those beliefs at the core, you'll never be able to make it fully to the next step.

Section 4

# Awareness and Choice

## Chapter 16

### *Learning What Controls You*

We seem to have the false belief we are in control of our life and we are actively engaged in every decision we make throughout our day, when the opposite is actually the truth. I've heard the statement that during any given day, we are not fully conscious of what we are doing 80-90% of the time. During that time, we are being driven by our subconscious. At first this may be hard to believe, but as you start being more aware, you will find out for yourself how much of your day is ruled by your subconscious. You will start to realize most of us are pretty much living our life on autopilot and most of the time you are not present in your current situation. Most of the time, you will find yourself thinking about what you did earlier or what you will or should be doing. You find that you are rarely in the present moment. As you start to become more aware of this, you will notice most of the time you are actually reacting to things based on what you were taught or programmed in the past, instead of living in the current situation.

I talked in previous chapters about how this programming occurs. Now I'm going to talk about how this programming can keep you from living in the present moment. I will discuss how it affects your daily life and keeps you reacting based on beliefs and thoughts you were taught in the past. Most books and lectures on growth focus on the need to be present. So how do you become present?

The first step to becoming present is becoming aware that you aren't present most of the time, but instead are living each moment based on your past programming and beliefs. What does it mean to be present? Being present means that instead of reacting to triggers and situations based on what happened to you in your past, you act and respond appropriately based upon what's happening currently in your life.

Begin by taking some time throughout your day to simply notice how much of your life you are living on "autopilot" or going through a routine. Take notice of your morning routine. You probably don't think about what you are doing as you go through your routine in the morning. You get out of bed and follow your routine without thinking. You might go to the bathroom first, then let out your dog or wake up your children, turn on the TV, make coffee, brush your teeth, etc. Do you make your bed when you get up or do you leave it? Do you have your clothes set out the night before? When do you pack your lunch? You have your routine and you're just going through the motions. That routine carries on to getting ready for work and leaving for work. Generally, when people arrive at work, they don't remember the drive there. That's what I mean by living on autopilot.

Being present means you notice the world around you when you're driving to work. It's living each moment fully. Did you notice the trees on the way in? Did it snow last night? If so, did you notice the beauty and wonder of the snow, or were you complaining because it slowed you down? Either way, it's at least being in the present. It's when you get to work and you don't even remember half the drive there... that's when you know that you weren't even really in the car while it was driving down the road. You were just kind of a passenger and someone else was driving the car. Who is this other person? What is this other thing that is running your life? Some people call it the ego; I like to call it the false self. It's the part of you that has been programmed or has learned the routine so well that it is actually running your life for you.

I used driving as an example of being on autopilot, but anytime you are going through the motions instead of being in the moment, you are on autopilot. You are on autopilot when you are following the programming I discussed earlier in this book. Autopilot is reacting based on what you were taught was appropriate for a given situation, instead of acting on what you really feel or believe.

Because most people can relate to it, I like to use learning to drive as a way to explain and illustrate programming and not being present, or acting on "autopilot." When you first learn to drive, you really have to put a lot of thought into it. You do your classroom learning, where you talk about the proper distance to follow another car, when to use your turn signal, who gets the right of way at stop signs, and all the proper etiquette of driving. Then you start the practical learning, driving the car with an instructor who corrects you when you make a mistake and furthers your knowledge of the rules of driving.

At first, you're pretty nervous about making mistakes and it takes a lot of conscious thought to put all the actions together. But with more practice, it becomes easier as you learn the rules of the road. Pretty soon you're driving without even thinking about it at the conscious level. Before you know it, you are on autopilot, driving down the road and thinking about other things. You don't have to consciously think about what you are doing.

It's the same thing with all of your programming: what you have been taught is now controlling you. You really don't consciously think about a lot of your actions throughout the day. You were taught by your family, your community, your country, things like: which side you are supposed to walk or drive on; how to shake hands; what language to speak; what each word means. You were taught what was considered "normal" or "right" for every action and detail of your life. For example, you were taught what trustworthy people look like and what suspicious ones look like. You were taught to judge people based on their sex, their color, how they wear their hair, what job they have, and so forth.

It took a while to learn to do this, just like it took time to learn all the rules that apply to driving. But, before long, you act and you judge people automatically, based on what you were taught. You, like everyone else, are walking around on autopilot. You have been taught how you are supposed to react and respond. More than likely you were taught by means of the reward and punishment model. If you reacted or responded the way you were taught, you were rewarded; if you reacted or responded incorrectly, you were disciplined.

To start to uncover your true self, you need to look at each of your beliefs to see if it is something you truly believe or if it is a belief you took on from your upbringing. This is how you can determine what is controlling you; this is an essential step in taking control of your own life and starting to live from your truth in the present moment. To start this process, just start to take notice of all the voices in your head. Those are the voices of everything you were taught and you will hear different voices in every situation. It can be somewhat overwhelming when you start to notice all the constant chatter going on in your head. You may want to start doing this for just short sessions and gradually increase how long you do it at any given time.

As an example, consider what might occur at a social gathering. You walk in and look around at the various people who are there. As you notice someone who is dressed very nicely, you hear a judgmental voice say, "I can't believe Tom wore something like that to this type of gathering. That's way overdressed." Then another voice comes up, one that's worried and anxious, and all of a sudden you're worried that maybe you should have dressed up a little more, maybe it's you who is underdressed. "Why didn't someone tell me that I was supposed to dress that nicely? What are people going to think?" Then you have a voice come out in anger, "Well, Susie should have told me what I was expected to wear when she told me about this gathering." And then your victim voice speaks up, "This always happens to me. I'm always the last one to know and I never get all of the information correctly. Now I'm going to look like a fool and everyone's going to hate me." And on and on the voices go. It is really amazing how much noise is always going on in your mind.

Each of us has all of these voices in our head. If we aren't aware of them, then they are what drives us and makes our decisions every day. These voices are usually driving, and driven themselves, by the fear of making a mistake. To become more present, you need to uncover— layer by layer, situation by situation—all the judgments and everything you have been taught, and find out for yourself whether what you uncover is your truth or a lie. This is a lifelong process and you start it just one situation at a time.

Here's how you go about this uncovering process. When you enter a situation, notice all of the voices in your head and just center your attention on one of them. As you hear that voice make a judgment or state a belief, focus on it. Ask yourself, "Where did I learn this belief?" Ask with curiosity and just wait for an answer to come up. You may get a clear picture of a time when an adult, peer, or teacher told you this belief. Then ask yourself if the belief is one that's true to you. Remember to feel into your body as you do this. If you have practiced the exercise that helps you feel the changes in your body when you are lying and when you are telling the truth, you will have an easier time determining if this is a truth for you or not. If you haven't practiced this, do so; it will make this process much easier.

You may find that this belief you have uncovered is a truth of yours or that it is something taught to you but not really your truth. For example, you might notice that you get anxious about what clothes you wear and that you wish you could wear what feels good to you instead of worrying about what everyone else will think. Through this experience, you have uncovered a belief that controls you, one that determines your choice of clothing based on what you believe others will think. Now, with your newfound awareness of that belief, you have a choice about how to go forward, about what to do and what you can change.

Once you get started with this, it gets easier and easier to find things that control you. One sure sign that you're being controlled by an uncovered thought or belief is when you have said, "I'm never going to do that again!" and then you find yourself doing it again. Another indication is when you find you get upset whenever you are around a particular person. No matter how hard you try, every time you are around that person, you end up getting angry and losing your temper. When you notice your consistent reaction to being around this person, you've gained an awareness of something you'd like to change. You would like to be able to stay calm around this person instead of reacting and letting your anger take over. All of these are indicators that you are not in control, that you have a trigger that causes a reaction, a reaction you often want to change but can't. The trigger pulls you out of the present moment. Your programming or a situation from your past is driving you.

Having the awareness is the first step. The change that allows you to remain present can take time to occur. To become fully present, you need to uncover the beliefs and past situations (programming) that cause you to react, heal that, and then choose to act a different way. Let's return to the driving example to illustrate how change can take time. If you learned to drive your car in the United States, you learned to follow all of the rules of driving on the right-hand side of the road. If all of a sudden you're transplanted to England, it's going to take some time to learn all of the rules—*new* rules to you—for driving on the left-hand side of the road. In the meantime, as you are getting used to driving on the left-hand side of the road, you'll likely find you tend to pull out onto the right-hand side of the road (the wrong side, in this situation) whenever you're not thinking, or when you get a little stressed or confused, or when your autopilot takes over. The process is the same any time your awareness leads you to want to change your reactions. It will take some time for the new way of acting to become normal to you.

Throughout this section, I'm going to talk about how to become aware of triggers and their controlling effects, and then how you can begin to change so you can start to live based on your own truth and your own values. As you follow this process, you'll find that some of the things you learned growing up are really your truths and you'll hang on to those. You'll also find that you don't want to hang on to some of the things you were taught; this is how you start to become more and more present.

As I said before, you begin by realizing that the majority of the things you do on a daily basis are reactions coming from your programming. You rarely make active choices based on the moment at hand. As you become more aware, you can start to make choices about how you truly want to live. To do this, you need to uncover your beliefs and see if each one is really your truth. When you start finding yourself judging something, just ask yourself, "Where did that belief come from?" For example, suppose you look at a man with long hair and the first thought that comes to your head is that men are supposed to have short hair. This is a judgment and it may or may not be your truth. Ask yourself these questions: "Where did that belief come from and is that a truth of mine? Does that feel right to me?"

Using this approach, you will start the process of uncovering the thoughts and feelings around any of your beliefs. This is a good way to begin forming an idea of where and how you got some of your programming. This approach will also guide you to recognizing your emotional responses and reactions. You can use your triggers—the things in your life that cause you to react—as your guides. I'll discuss this in the next chapter and also talk about how you can use these triggers to help yourself become more present in your daily life.

## Chapter 17

*Using Triggers as Guides*

What is a trigger? A trigger is anything that causes a reaction in you. What is reacting? It's when you are reliving something that happened in your past and it's controlling you in the present. Sometimes people misunderstand growing, and becoming more present and true to yourself, to mean that you will no longer have any emotional responses. The acts of healing and growing should not be about controlling your emotions; they should actually lead you to feel more deeply touched by life than ever!

Some triggers bring up feelings you like. These triggers reveal areas in which you have grown or show you characteristics in others that you would like to have in yourself. Other triggers show you parts of yourself that need to heal or grow. By developing your awareness, you learn to recognize when you are reacting in a way that is not true to you in your current situation. This awareness can be shown to you by a trigger that causes you to react in a way that feels hurtful to yourself or to others. These are the times when it seems you are being "taken over" and become a bystander in your own life. You all know what I'm talking about!

Here's an example of a trigger that causes you to react in a way that feels hurtful to yourself or to others. Someone comes up to you and makes a comment, and you find yourself going off on the person, totally overreacting to the current situation. You have been triggered. Something the person says in the present triggers a hurt from the past or triggers the eruption of an emotional volcano. In this example, the comment triggered emotions you had buried and tried to hide, causing an emotionally charged reaction. Look at the word *react*: you act out something in the present moment that happened in the past.

Again, I am not saying you shouldn't feel or express emotions, or that emotions are bad. If you see a child being mistreated, expressing anger is very appropriate. The following situation is an example of overreacting. Suppose someone walks up to you and says out of the blue, "Oh, where'd you get that coat?" Hearing this, your internal voices go wild. You are suddenly overtaken by these beliefs: this person doesn't like your coat; this person is implying your coat's not good enough and that's a comment about you too; you're not good enough because of the coat you're wearing. You find yourself raising your voice and saying angrily, "It's none of your business where I got this coat. I like this coat and that's all there is to it!" In a case like this, the person who asked you the question will probably look very confused and wonder what just happened.

As you consider the preceding example, it may seem funny and yet you probably can relate to it too. We all get triggered. But, incidents in which we are triggered are not usually funny at the time and can lead to misunderstandings and hurt. Afterwards, we usually feel bad for the way we responded and want to try to avoid acting that way again. This is how something that triggers a response we do not like can lead us to growth. Triggers show us the places in ourselves that pull us out of the present moment. These are places that need healing so we can become present. How can you use triggers to help with your growth? You can grow by letting yourself feel under the triggers and by not blaming the person who triggers you. I will get into the details of feeling into the triggers in the next chapter.

As you start to notice and observe the various triggers in your life, you are likely to find this process can bring up some of your most powerful false beliefs and show you the places where you have stored emotions that need to be felt and released. On the flip side, I also want you to notice the triggers that help you feel sensations and emotions that are pleasant, the triggers that bring up joy and happiness. Allow yourself to really feel the pleasant feelings too, because it can get easy to focus only on what you want to change. You want to balance looking at what you want to change with appreciating what has already changed.

Another important part of your healing journey is taking time to appreciate the areas in your life with which you are happy. Focusing only on the things you would like to change, or the things you do not like, keeps you from appreciating all of your growth and wonderful aspects. To help see the value of nurturing and appreciating, consider the example of a garden. If you want a beautiful garden, you do more than just focus on pulling the weeds. You also make sure the soil is fertile, you plant what you want to grow in your garden, and you take time to water and fertilize the plants. We want to do the same thing in our journey to heal. What do you want to grow? What are you planting in your garden (your soul, body, and spirit)? Are you nurturing yourself? What are you eating? What are your thoughts? When you notice things that trigger joy and happiness, make an effort to bring more of that into your life. Nourish your spirit.

I am sure you have heard the statement that the things you don't like in others are a reflection of the things you don't like in yourself. When you are triggered by someone's behavior because you are afraid that behavior could be yours, the person is exhibiting traits you fear may be yours too. For instance, if you see someone and perceive them to be stuck in sorrow or anger, and it triggers you, it's because you are afraid to be stuck and it scares you. If you see someone completely shut down in life and completely full of fears, you may find yourself repelled by them, or even become angry with them easily, because you are afraid of what they represent. This is the same reason why so many people are afraid of or pretend not to notice homeless people. Deep down, they know: That could be me. One of our biggest fears is to be homeless and alone, to have "lost it all." Most people want to imagine all homeless people are deranged or lazy, which is why they became homeless. We make ourselves think of the reasons why someone is homeless because it's too scary to think that could be us.

One part of growth is learning to notice the triggers that bring up the kinds of responses we would like to change. However, I also want to encourage you to notice the triggers that bring up parts you want to nurture. Pull the weeds, and *also* water and fertilize the flowers. Notice the parts in you that you want to blossom even more fully, the qualities you like and want to expand upon. You need to spend as much time noticing these things as the ones you want to change, because appreciation and gratitude are necessary in the growth process. These make up the fertilizer that will be immensely helpful to you in your growth.

Always focusing on what you don't like about yourself just helps reinforce those beliefs that you're not good enough, that you're not worthy. We are all completely worthy and good enough. As I stated earlier, when you see ugliness or fear in others, it's a reflection of what is in you. It's also true that when you see beauty, grace, and love in others, these are also a reflection of what is within you. When you see a quality you really admire in someone else, the only way you can recognize that quality is that it is in you also. Take time to notice the attributes you admire in others and would like to nurture in yourself. Be around people and things that touch your heart and soul with beauty. It can be getting out in nature, appreciating art, listening to beautiful music, listening to the waves on the beach, spending time with people you love. Make time to do the things in your life that help bring you joy and help reconnect you to beauty and love. When you do this, joy and beauty and love can become a bigger part of your life. This is how you help your body, spirit, and soul to reveal the beauty within you.

## Chapter 18

*Feeling the Trigger*

This chapter addresses one of the most important parts of healing: feeling your way through triggers to growth. You will find I repeat myself through this chapter, bringing up points I have made previously and also repeating points several times in this chapter. This is not a mistake. I have done this because it can take repetition to bring about true understanding. Each time you come across a point again, take time to let it go through the phases of understanding. First, you will have an intellectual understanding of the concept. As you stay with it and start to apply it, you will work toward getting a felt understanding. This is when it is no longer an idea, but an actual truth. It is important to take the time to make this transition, from an intellectual understanding to a felt understanding or truth. Otherwise it will just be another interesting concept you are unable to apply to growth and healing.

When you find yourself triggered in a way that causes a reaction that you want to improve—like in the example of the coat in the previous chapter—how do you shift to letting that trigger guide you to healing? How do you feel your way through that? It can be hard for you in the situation to do much more than hang on for the ride. Once you can step back and observe—and this may not happen until after you have left the situation or even hours, days, or years later—you can do some reflecting and uncover what is under the reaction.

Let's return to the coat example and observe a trigger and some responses. Note your first response may be to blame the other person. "How dare they ask me where I got my coat?!" Blaming others for your reactions will never lead to growth. It may feel good, as it's easier to blame others than to look inside at your own hurts, but it will not lead to growth. When you find yourself triggered, try to remember to let go of the *why* questions. If you ask, "Why did I react that way?" you will only get into your head and go down the path of trying to find a logical answer, instead of letting your feelings guide you to healing. If you want to grow, you need to get out of your head and use the triggers to help you feel under the initial reaction to the true cause of the reaction. Often, the path you find yourself on will take you places you "never would have thought of."

Instead of asking "Why did I react that way?" you need to feel what the reaction brought up. Feel what it felt like when the person asked you, "Where did you get that coat?" Ask yourself what being asked that question felt like. What emotions or other sensations did that question bring up? Then take time and feel each of the sensations that come up. If the question brought up anger, then feel the anger. Let yourself really feel the anger, and, as you do this, see if you have any reaction in your body. You may have a definite response, like your stomach tightening, or your jaw clenching, or your shoulders rising. This is telling you where your body physically responds when you have this reaction. This may be a place where tissue memory of this trigger is stored; it may be one that will eventually develop physical wearing associated with these sensations. You'll often be able to feel exactly where the sensation sits in your body.

After you have taken time to really sit with the feelings brought up in the initial response— anger in this example—now it's time to see if there is anything under this. You could ask yourself, "Is there anything under the anger?" or "What do I feel under the anger?" There may not be anything else to feel. It may be that this buildup of anger may be what you needed to express. But, there are often more layers to feel through. As you feel in more deeply, the next thing that may come up is the way you felt when you took the comment to mean you "aren't good enough." With each layer, you need to take the time to feel what comes up and where your body might be storing or reacting to what comes up. To take this to the core, you need to keep asking questions which help you uncover the layers. To continue with this example, you might ask the question "When else in my life have I ever felt or believed that I wasn't good enough?" or set the intention "Let me feel all the times I felt that I wasn't good enough." To get to the core, you might also ask "When is the first time that I ever felt that I wasn't good enough?"

Continue to do this and work down through the layers of sensations, thoughts, emotions, and beliefs. This is how you can use the triggers to lead you to healing. Doing so can bring up some very intense sensations and hurts you thought had been healed or forgotten. The key is to notice when you are trying to think of an answer as opposed to when you are letting go of the need to know why and just feeling what comes up. Where this leads you may not be reasonable and is not usually linear, and this is why it is important to let go of the need to know why or to make sense out of what you are feeling. You may not have a cognitive memory of what is driving these reactions. You will have a felt sense of it though. As you feel down into the tissue and let these feelings come up, sometimes a memory comes up. At other times, all that may come up is intense sensation or emotion; you may not know the cause and it may be that just feeling and expressing whatever comes up is all you need to do to heal. At other times, you may feel a spot in your body that is tight or knotted up. If you do, that place may need some physical treatment before you can release fully the emotions, thoughts, and beliefs controlling you.

As you are allowing yourself to feel your responses to the trigger, you may actually get a very clear visualization of a time in your life when you first felt this way. You may see yourself at a previous time interacting with another person who is telling you that you are not good enough and recognize it as the time when you took on this belief. Sometimes you'll get a very clear picture of the situation and have had no memory of it until that very moment. If this is the case, you need to feel all the sensations and beliefs around this situation to help yourself heal. As you let yourself feel through to healing, you can truly stop being ruled by these situations in your past. This process of feeling down to the core may happen quickly, or it can take hours, days, months, or years to get completely to the core of some triggers. Remember not to rush or force. The process will unfold as it is supposed to do. Your part is to keep being open to go deeper into the feelings as they come up.

In the following chapters, I discuss some ways to connect with the younger parts of you and help come to healing. It starts with just feeling what comes up and being open to choosing a healthier belief and believing that you can heal. You can do this by using your triggers to guide you down to the core places, the places where the false beliefs literally became a part of your body. If you are in your head and caught in the cycle of thinking, you are not at the level of the problem! Changing your thoughts is very important, but until you uncover the core of the problem, you will continue to find yourself fighting the same reactions again and again. How do you know when you have healed to the core? When you find yourself in a situation that would normally trigger you, and you are no longer triggered. How do you know what you need to still work on and heal? Just see what triggers you!

These triggers end up controlling us and rule our lives. In the example of the coat, the person actually may have been coming up to you to give you a compliment. But, when you have negative beliefs in your tissues—I'm not good enough; I'm not worthy; I'm stupid; I deserve to be hurt; etc.—those beliefs control you. So even when someone tries to give you a compliment, you will turn it around into a put down. And no matter how many times you give yourself positive affirmations—I am good enough; I deserve to be loved; etc.—the negative beliefs buried deep inside you rule you and prevent you from believing the positives.

The negative beliefs rule your sub-consciousness and no matter what you try to change or what you say in your head, you can't change your reaction until you feel through to the core of the reaction. To heal and to change these negative beliefs controlling you, let your triggers and feelings guide you. It's pretty easy to find out what you need to work on next: follow your triggers. If you keep having a lot of anger or sorrow triggered, or if you keep having people come into your life that bring up the same reactions again and again, then that's what you need to feel through.

I mentioned earlier that blaming others for your reactions will never lead to healing. The truth is no one can make you feel a particular way if you don't already feel that way because of something *you* believe. I heard the following statement and it is true: "No one can make you feel stupid without your consent." The same is true if you substitute other words for stupid: unworthy, unlovable, a failure, etc. I love how Wayne Dyer described this in one of his books. I paraphrase here what he said and also what I remember of an example he gave.

He used the example of a woman coming into him for counseling. Her main complaint was that her husband makes her feel stupid. He asked her how it was that her husband was able to make her feel stupid. The woman's response was that her husband said things and acted in ways that made her feel like she was stupid. Wayne responds, "So, if you're husband tells you you're a car, do you believe him?" The woman instantly responded, "No!" Wayne goes on to say, "Now really, if your husband tells you you're a car and he wants you to get around on the floor and make noises like a car because you are a car, are you going to believe him?" The woman responds that it would be crazy because she isn't a car. Wayne responded, "Then how can he make you feel stupid?"

You have to believe what someone says for it to be true. It doesn't matter how many times someone tells you that you are stupid; if you don't believe you are stupid, what the person says will not affect you. The same is true of compliments. It doesn't matter how much someone says they love you; if you don't believe you are lovable, you won't believe them.

Here's another example of how this works. Suppose someone comes up to you out of nowhere and, being as mean as they could possibly be, full of anger and self-righteousness, yells at you, "You are blue and you shouldn't be blue! You are the color blue and no one should be that color!" You know you are not blue, so it doesn't cause you to react. You can look at the person calmly and say, "Well, if you want to believe that, then that's your issue." Saying that, you let what the person said have no effect on you. On the other hand, suppose someone walks up to you and says, "You are so worthless. You are the most worthless person on the face of the earth." If there's any part of you that believes you're worthless, the person's comment will trigger your reactions to feeling worthless. If you know to your core you are a very wonderful, worthy person, anyone's comments to the contrary can't affect you.

Each of these hypothetical situations provides an example of a trigger. A trigger is anything—something someone says or does, some situation in your life—that causes a response or reaction in you, one you really can't control and do not usually like to feel. For instance, your reaction to a trigger might be experiencing feelings of not being good enough, not being worthy, not deserving love. When a trigger occurs, it is showing you a place you need to heal if you want to be your true self fully. So, for instance, if you want to believe in love fully, to believe you are loveable, you need to uncover the places within you where you've taken on falsehoods that keep you from believing in love and in your being loveable.

Let's return to a previous example, one completely different from the emotional response to a comment made about the coat. Recall the hypothetical car accident in which someone runs a stop sign and broadsides you in your car. Now, whenever you approach an intersection while you're driving and see another vehicle coming from the other direction, you immediately feel yourself start to brace. This reaction happens without your thinking about it, and you cannot stop it from happening. This is another example of being controlled by a trigger stemming from a past trauma. No matter how many times you tell yourself you're safe and you don't need to brace, the reaction happens. You can't control the reaction in your mind.

This is another trigger you can follow through to uncover and heal. Obviously, when the triggering situation arises while you're driving down the road, you can't just stop in the middle of the road and do some deep breathing to uncover the core; you might cause another accident. However, when the triggering situation occurs, you *can* start to be aware of your reaction and to feel the place(s) in your body where you brace and tighten. Later, when you are safe and can lie down, you can visualize the same situation—driving toward an intersection controlled by stop signs and seeing a car approaching from the opposite direction—and create the same responses in your body. Visualizing this, you can now take the time to really feel what is happening and treat the areas that are tight. You can also feel the emotions that may come up and allow yourself to heal. Set a goal of seeing yourself come to an intersection and staying relaxed. I will discuss setting goals in Chapter 20 and go into detail about how setting goals can help uncover areas that need to be healed.

A trigger is anything that controls you. You cannot stop it mentally. It's a reaction that takes you over when it occurs. It's a piece of you that is no longer in the present moment. Triggers manifest in many different forms; they can come from people, situations, sounds, smells. Fears can often become so overpowering that you have difficulty controlling them. For instance, consider someone who is claustrophobic. When in an enclosed space, he can't simply tell himself he is okay. He feels the room trapping him and there's nothing he can say in his mind or do to change that feeling. He is controlled by the reactions triggered by enclosed places. As you become more aware of your own triggers, and start to feel your way through them, you can uncover your true self and live more in the present moment.

Chapter 19

*Forgiveness*

As you feel these triggers and follow them down to the core, it may lead you to an incident that involved another person and that person may have been the cause of the emotional or physical trauma you experienced. This is where forgiveness comes into the healing process. You might have had a car accident. Perhaps you uncover a time when a family member or friend acted in a way that caused you to feel betrayed or not good enough. You might recall an incident in which you or a loved one was physically injured or abused. Whatever the situation, you may feel that you can never get over it or that you will never be able to forgive the other person.

Sooner or later, as you work through healing, you will come to a point where forgiveness is necessary for the next step to take place. It may be a matter of forgiving someone else or forgiving yourself. Forgiveness is one of the most important steps along the path of healing and for some people it is the hardest part of the entire journey. The concept of right and wrong is the biggest stumbling block to forgiveness. Many people believe forgiving someone is the same as saying that what happened was "okay" or that it was "right."

*Forgiveness has nothing to do with right or wrong; it has to do with taking your power back.* As long as you blame or have anger towards another person, they have power over you. When you learn to forgive, you empower yourself. When you forgive someone for something you feel they've done against you that caused you hurt or trauma, you are actually taking your power back in the situation. If you hold onto blame, hold on to feeling that what was done to you was wrong or should not have happened, there's no way to move forward. As long as you hold on in this way, that situation or that person has essential power over you. The situation or person controls you every moment of every day.

Forgiveness is about releasing. To forgive is to release the power from the situation or person that led you to hold on to the feelings arising from trauma and to bring all of your power back into you. Various situations, traumas, and trials are brought into our lives not to punish us but to help us in one way or another, to help us grow or learn a lesson. When I use the word lesson, I don't mean you did something wrong and you had to learn a lesson. I mean you learn a lesson that brings about growth. Things happen in our lives to help us grow and reach the next level of our spiritual development.

A friend of mine described this in a way that really helped bring clarity to this subject. She had read an article that asked people to describe life. There was a variety of answers. Life is a circus. Life is hard. Life is a party. When my friend considered her description of life, what came to her was "Life is necessary" and "Life is important." Life is necessary for us to grow spiritually. In our lives, we will have times of abundance, of love, of passion. These times are necessary for us to learn how to receive, how to feel joy, and to appreciate these experiences and the times when they occur. There will also be times when we have pain, loss, sorrow, scarcity. These times are necessary for us to learn lessons too. Some of these, among many others, may be lessons in appreciating even the small things or in knowing we are always loved. The "good" times aren't a reward and the "bad" times aren't a punishment. All aspects of life are necessary for our souls to grow. And all aspects of life are important. Remembering this can be very freeing.

Colin Tippin's *Radical Forgiveness* goes into this approach to forgiveness in much more detail than do I in this one chapter. Colin has written several books and has also made several CDs that offer more information on forgiveness. *Radical Forgiveness* is easy to read and understand, and it goes into the concept of looking beyond just the current situation and getting to any issues the situation may be triggering. I will discuss going beyond the current situation, letting go of the right and wrong mentality, and getting to a deeper healing in this chapter. His book goes into much more specific details since the entire book is dedicated to forgiveness. He also has a worksheet that is a helpful tool in working through to forgiveness.

When you find yourself asking questions like "Why is this happening to me again?" or "How come this always seems to happen to me?" this is an indication you have an area that needs to be uncovered and healed. The same is true when you find yourself in similar situations again and again. At these times, using Colin's worksheet can be a helpful way to feel through to the root of the issue. The worksheet gives you a way to step back, detach from the situation, write about the current situation as you see it, and then open up to forgiveness or another perspective. As you go through the worksheet, let yourself feel all the emotions that come up. Take time to stop as needed and really feel and express whatever you feel is needed. As you do this, if you can be open—even just a little bit—to the idea that this situation keeps happening to help you grow in some way, you will be ready to work on acceptance and forgiveness.

As I stated earlier, the only way to move toward healing and forgiveness is to get out of the mindset that the situation shouldn't be or shouldn't have happened. If you can do this, you can break free from the "blame game" that inevitably stops you from forgiving. This is a much easier concept to accept when dealing with the simple, day-to-day situations that warrant forgiveness than it is in more emotionally charged situations. You will probably find it easier to start practicing forgiveness in these less charged situations, and that will help you work up to the more difficult or emotionally charged situations. Starting with the less charged situations, you will be able to see how forgiveness can be so powerful in the more difficult situations too.

If you keep finding yourself having a similar problem come up in various relationships—the names of the people involved may keep changing but the way you're being treated stays the same—that is a good indication you are being asked to investigate and heal something within yourself. If you find that in many of your interactions—whether with your spouse, boss, co-worker, or even the mail carrier—you keep finding the same feeling being triggered in you, this is something to explore. The feeling you need to address could be anything, but it is one you don't like. For example, you may feel you are stupid, or disrespected, or disregarded. You might go on and on without seeing the pattern of triggering, but if you take the time to notice these triggers, you will see the only common denominator in all these situations is you. If you keep blaming others, then the situations will keep occurring. If you take time to heal yourself, then you will no longer need to have these situations in your life. Situations that trigger you continue to happen in order to show you a place within yourself that needs to heal.

To find the place these situations keep pointing out needs healing in you, you will need to take the time to feel under the current situation to the core. Feel how the situation makes you feel, as you let go of the blame. If you find yourself saying "I feel disrespected" then really let yourself feel all the times you have felt that way. Take your time and really feel all the layers of the feeling. This may take quite a bit of time and may bring up a lot of emotions of which you weren't even aware. Then let yourself see if there are any feelings under what you have uncovered so far. When you do this, it might lead to other feelings, one like not being good enough or not being worthy of love.

As you continue to feel the layers of feelings releasing, you might ask yourself to connect to the first time you ever felt that way. This is what will help you get to the core of what is making you feel this way. You may see a scene from your past or you may just feel emotions. What comes up doesn't matter; you just need to feel it and give it a way out of you. This is the key to complete healing: feel to the core of the feeling and then let it go; uncover all the subconscious beliefs, thoughts, and traumas controlling you. Until you heal completely, you will continue to draw people and situations into your life to trigger these subconscious areas. Once you forgive fully and heal, the triggers will be gone. At that time, you will begin to draw people and situations into your life that will meet you at this new level.

The kinds of situations I've mentioned so far can be very emotional, but they are much easier to move through to forgiveness than situations in which people have been significantly injured or killed, whether by accident or deliberate attack. How do you forgive someone when you are so caught up in feeling that the person did something wrong that shouldn't have happened? Anytime you lose a loved one, you will have a mourning and grieving process to work through. Unfortunately, people often get stuck in the process because they get caught in the belief that the loss of that loved one should not have happened. It can really be hard if you hold onto beliefs that go against the laws of nature. Losing someone can be painful even that person lived what is considered a long and full life. We grieve for the loss of our loved one's physical presence in our lives.

But, the belief no one should ever die "before their time" causes a lot of suffering. Who determines when someone has lived "long enough?" I am sure you have heard it said that a child should never die before the parent does. This belief does not follow the laws of nature and can really prevent people from healing. If you look at nature, a long life is not guaranteed; young animals die frequently. While losing anyone you love can be painful, believing that young people shouldn't die makes the process of forgiveness and healing much more difficult. Holding this belief can lead to getting caught in the cycle of thinking, "If I had only done this" or "I should have done that," a cycle that keep you stuck in the past and keeps you from the grace of love and healing.

Moving through the stages of mourning, acceptance, and forgiveness is a process. As you work through this process, you may encounter a variety of emotions and beliefs, and some of them may be very strong. Some of these emotions might be sadness, sorrow, anger, rage, or fear. Some of the beliefs might be that the loss shouldn't have happened, that you can never heal, that you shouldn't be happy or enjoy life anymore. As you work through these emotions and beliefs, be gentle with yourself and allow yourself time to feel fully through each of them. Remember healing is an active process and keep moving forward.

Opening up to forgiveness is a way to keep the process moving forward toward healing. As you work to forgive, you may also start to accept. As you allow yourself to step outside of judging the situation to be wrong and move towards the belief that these things happen for your spiritual growth, you move toward healing. You can start to move forward even if you truly believe that nothing good can or will ever come from what happened. As long as you are open to the possibility that you may someday be able to forgive, you can move forward.

Let go of expectations that this will be an instantaneous healing. It can take time to work through all the layers of emotions and beliefs. People who have a really strong connection to the belief that there is a purpose for every situation—even if that purpose doesn't make reasonable sense in our human terms—tend to be able to move more quickly into the stage of forgiveness and acceptance. On the other hand, people who have a deep grip on the false belief that good people are rewarded and bad people are punished have a much harder time reaching a state of forgiveness in a situation in which a person perceived as "good" was punished, hurt, or abused.

The events in our lives have nothing to do with being rewarded or punished. To believe that would be to believe that rain falls only on flowers and never on weeds, or that only bad trees are struck by lightning. The situations that challenge us, that trigger us, occur in our lives to help us grow into our own potential and to help all of humanity evolve and grow. How all this works goes way beyond what we can understand with our limited reasoning and our beliefs, especially when we have the false belief that only bad people are punished or only bad people have bad things happen to them. This is another belief that causes a lot of suffering. If you are deeply entrenched in this belief, then the idea of forgiveness—especially in the situation where a young child is killed by a drunk driver—can seem impossible to you. If you continue to choose to cling to this belief, your choice might leave you stuck in a state of suffering for the rest of your life. Suffering occurs from resisting the acceptance of what is. Saying something shouldn't have happened keeps you completely in that state of suffering and hurt.

This is what I mean when I say that forgiveness doesn't have anything to do with the other person in a situation or whether the situation was right or wrong. Forgiveness has to do with letting go. Forgiveness is not about trying to understand why something happened. If you can be open to the possibility that there is some reason that the situation occurred—even though the reason may be way beyond your understanding—then the progression toward healing can occur, even if you don't understand it right now. As soon as you open yourself up even slightly to that possibility, the grace of forgiveness and healing can occur in your life.

Often, we are unable to forgive others because we are unable to forgive ourselves for things that occurred in our lives. We continue to punish ourselves for things that happened years ago. Sometimes we're not even consciously aware that we're doing it. I've seen this come up many times during treatments in which a client's tissue memory is triggered and brings up childhood trauma. For example, during treatment memories of rape or molestation may surface, and, even though someone clearly forced themselves on the client, the client may have taken on the belief that it was their own fault or that they deserved it. This false belief is particularly likely when the client believes only "bad" people are punished or hurt.

Holding onto these beliefs can keep you from healing from the trauma of rape or molestation. You might have any number of false beliefs. "I shouldn't have walked down that street." "I shouldn't have worn that perfume." "I shouldn't have trusted that person even though my parents, friends, community members trust them." "I should've been able to fight off that person." The beliefs can go on and on. These beliefs can lead you to believe you deserve to be punished. If this is the case, you may keep drawing people who hurt you into your life because you believe you deserve to be punished.

If something like this comes up in your life, or if you have a situation for which you know you're still blaming yourself, then the way to help yourself move towards healing is to visualize being in the situation again. See yourself at the age you were at the time, and also see yourself at your present observing the scene. Then, let the scene unfold and feel what comes up. To heal, you need to help the younger version of you heal. Look the younger you fully in the eyes and feel what he or she is feeling at the time. Take the time to feel in yourself what is coming up for the younger you. Then visualize doing whatever needs to be done to help the younger you and to help him or her heal. You may need to step in and do battle with the abuser. You may need to remove the younger you from the situation; you may need to hold him or her. Many different situations may occur. Allow whatever situations arise to unfold and, as you do this, let yourself really feel.

Often, some part you wants to blame the younger you. To help yourself really heal, replace the younger you with someone you love and see that person in the same situation. This makes it easier to take a step back and ask if you would blame this loved one for this situation like you're blaming yourself. Most of the time when you look at someone else in your same situation, especially if it's someone you love, all the hate and blame dissolves. We are a lot harder on ourselves than we would ever be on anyone else. You can take this same approach when trying to forgive someone else. What if you were the person who had drunk too much, gotten behind the wheel, and ended up taking someone's life because of it?

Every step along the way, and every little bit you are able to forgive someone else or yourself, will allow healing to occur not only within you but within everyone who is or was involved in the situation. This is a process, and it can take time. However, don't trap yourself into the belief that it must take a long time, as huge shifts can happen in mere seconds. Allow yourself to feel as much as you can and to chip away at it. Sometimes you may experience small slivers of change; other times you may have a landslide occur. It can take a while for you to see that any of these things that happened could possibly lead to growth. Meet yourself with gentleness and be open to the possibility of moving into acceptance and forgiveness.

How do you know when you have fully forgiven yourself, someone else, or a situation? It's when you can talk truly and honestly about that situation and feel openness in your heart and peace in your soul. When you feel that way, you know that acceptance and forgiveness have occurred. If you feel yourself tightening or clenching, if you feel tears or anger bubbling up, if you feel a lump in your throat, those are signs you still have some layers needing your work. If so, it's okay; there may be many layers. Appreciate how much you have healed, and then keep moving forward.

Connecting into your body's reactions provides a good guide to knowing whether you have fully forgiven and fully healed in a situation. No one can make you forgive anyone. You can hold on to the hate and blame as long as you want to do so. Just keep the awareness that as long as you hold on to the hate and blame, you're hurting only yourself and not the person whom you blame. If you want to step back into your power and be truly free, work on forgiveness.

Chapter 20

*The Importance of Goals—*
*What Do You Want?*

The word "goal" provokes a variety of reactions. Some people see goals as a way to help themselves along their journey in life. These people have used goals as something to anticipate, something to work towards, to help them along their journey. Other people relate the word "goal" to a linear, step-by-step process that leaves no room for change. When thinking of goals, these people may focus on what they haven't achieved and where they have failed. Using goals to focus on what you haven't achieved can actually keep you small instead of helping you to expand and grow.

I am comfortable with the word goal and use it in my examples. I did have to take some time to go deeply into all of the thoughts and beliefs associated with goals. It took time to learn to see the goal process as a dynamic and changing process, instead of one of setting a specific goal and pushing until you reach that goal, pushing even when the goal no longer fits into your life. I had to let go of the idea that not obtaining a goal or changing a goal is a sign of failure. I now understand the goal process should actually be dynamic. Goals start you down a path. Once you are on that path, you will see all kinds of possible routes you didn't even know existed before you started down the path. You need to be dynamic as you go along your journey, and that includes being dynamic with your goals too. When you reach a new route, it's time to reevaluate and see if that route is now the way to go.

If you are not comfortable with the term goal, feel free to substitute a word that suits you better. Some people like to use the words intent or focus. A question I like to use when setting goals is "What do I want?" You want to focus on what you want in your life. Setting goals is a way to focus your energy on what you want and also to notice where you might be focusing on what you don't want. As with everything else in this book, use whatever words are comfortable for you. Also, remember that if the word "goal" brings up a reaction in you, you need to take the time to go into and explore that reaction. Doing this can help you by freeing any negative or blocked ideas about what goals can be, leaving you to focus more fully on expanding and growing.

At one of his seminars, John F. Barnes compared setting a goal with putting up a sail in a sailboat and choosing a direction. I really like that analogy and have expanded on it to help with my understanding of the goal setting process. Sometimes, when I ask people to set a goal, they say they just want to let life unfold the way it's meant to unfold and that goals are too linear or controlling. That's like sitting out in the middle of the ocean, letting the waves take you wherever they might, and you not doing your part, which includes putting up the sail. The goal process is a balance of doing your part and then trusting that the universe will give you what you need. It is also about sensing when you would do better to change directions (change or revise your goal). I will use the sailing analogy to illustrate how essential it is that the goal setting process be dynamic.

When you set out sailing, you may not be quite sure where you want to go. You sit in the boat with your sail down, taking time to reflect and to open up to guidance. Once the guidance comes, it's up to you to set the course and put up the sail. You have to move into action. Some people don't act at this point; because they are afraid that they'll go the wrong direction, they don't put up the sail. Some people are so afraid of making mistakes they will choose to ignore guidance, staying passive instead and going wherever the tide takes them. These same people will often judge and ridicule those who do set their sails and head out. They will also complain about their life, even though it's their choice to keep the sail down.

Now is the time to take action. If you want to change, then pick a course. Make a goal. Then just start moving and see where it goes. Life truly is like sailing. If you choose a direction definitely not meant for you, the wind won't let you go that way. If the universe really wants you to go in a certain direction, it will send the wind into that direction. So, no matter how hard you try to go the "wrong" way, you really can't. If the sail is up, no matter how hard you paddle against a blowing wind, it's going to take you the direction it wants you to go. Let go of the idea you could go the wrong direction or make a mistake, and trust the universe is going to help you go where you need to go. Often, the direction you think you are supposed to go and the one you are really meant to go are complete opposites.

You set a goal based on what you believe is supposed to happen and then put up your sail and the adventure begins. Maybe the wind is with you and you start going in your intended direction; you start thinking you picked the "right" direction. Then, all of a sudden the wind stops and you're just sitting there. You can see the island you picked, your goal, your destination. You are almost there, and then the wind changes direction. Now it's taking you away from your intended destination, from where you thought you needed to go.

When you're shifted away from your goal, you may well start to doubt that you made the "right" goal. You might become frustrated and wonder why you got so close, only to have your dream then "taken away." Being shifted away from your goal can cause you to doubt yourself, the goal, and often the universal force itself. When you begin to doubt, you may start to lose trust and faith. When you're hindered in your pursuit of a goal, it may be a question of how hard you're willing to work to achieve the goal. Sometimes struggle is involved. You will need to work. Are you willing to put in the necessary effort, even when it appears the world has turned against you? If so, you drop the sail and start to paddle.

After you paddle against it a while, the wind may shift back to your direction and help you again. It was just a test of trusting and you may end up at your original destination. Alternately, you might struggle and struggle, fighting against a wind that continues to take you in another direction. If this happens, it's a good time to re-evaluate, to quiet down and reconnect, to see if it's time to change your course. When you started out, you knew what you thought you wanted. Can you now be open to the possibility that you need to go to another place first, or that perhaps there's something else you need to learn or heal before you get to your chosen destination?

You can continue to struggle as much as you want, but the universe will still take you the way you are supposed to go. Sometimes you will have to exhaust yourself completely before you are willing to stop; other times you will stop before you manage to exhaust yourself. When you stop struggling, it's time to re-evaluate your plan and your goal, time to look at what's in the direction into which you're being moved. You may not like going in this new direction; it may not be where you think you're supposed to go, but all signs are pointing this way. At times you will struggle and collapse and struggle and collapse many times before you surrender to the direction you are meant to go. This part of the process may bring up your beliefs about making mistakes or failing. If so, you have the opportunity to consider whether there are healthier beliefs about living life, about mistakes and failures. In the end, you may find yourself going in a direction totally different from the one you first chose and on this new journey you may uncover treasures you would have missed going the other direction.

This very sort of thing happened to me while I was working for John F. Barnes at his Myofascial Release Center in Paoli, Pennsylvania. I had gotten my dream job! Like most people, I thought being able to work with John at one of his treatment centers would be a dream come true. I remember saying to myself at my first seminar with John, "Someday

I want to be good enough to work at one of his treatment centers." So here I was. I had obtained this. All of a sudden, I started feeling this uneasiness and had a calling that I was supposed to return to my hometown of Orland, Indiana. I fought this feeling for quite a while. I mean... this was my dream job. I had achieved my goal. Why would I be called to return to a very small town in the Midwest where no one even knew about myofascial release? What if I started a clinic and it failed? I had achieved my goal, one anyone would want, and now I had this calling to return home. I started really questioning myself and fighting that voice.

About that time, a friend of mine sent me a card that read, "On my way to my dream I got lost and found a better one." That card really touched me and helped me to re-evaluate. We sometimes get so caught up in our goal or our dream that we don't see the possibility of its being a stepping stone to another place. We can get so focused on a goal that we will continue along to that goal even though we have had many insights saying it's time to go another direction. Since I followed that call to return to my hometown, my life has gone in directions I never would have imagined. My clinic is extremely busy, and I have added using horses as a component to help people heal, something I had never considered would happen. It has become a wonderful healing center.

Another facet of the growth process is that you can't *miss* your opportunity. I know that if I hadn't listened to my calling and instead stayed at my job at John's Paoli clinic, the wind and waves would've forced me out. I would have been forced to leave eventually. I am sure you have heard of or known people who knew they needed to leave a job or relationship, but remained nevertheless out of fear. These people generally are fired from the job, forced out of the relationship. As I heard Carolyn Myss say, "You can either help steer the engine or get dragged along behind the caboose; but, either way, you will be taken the way you are meant to go!"

To return to the sailboat analogy for the goal process: do your part and allow the universe to do its part. When you are blown completely off course, remember this doesn't mean you were heading in the wrong direction; it just means it is time for a shift. You may have to go completely off your chosen path so you can learn, grow, or heal in ways that help you appreciate your path fully. You may need a detour and later end up heading back towards your original goal. Or, you may realize suddenly that you needed to learn everything you learned so that you could head down this other, new path, one which will take you to where you are truly meant to go. Don't look at goals as static and linear, but rather as dynamic and ever-changing, just like anything else in your life. Part of the goal process is to stop and re-evaluate periodically, to observe and access where you are now, how far you've come, and whether you feel you are meant to stay on the same course.

You might also find you are heading along nicely, and all the sudden, the wind dies. You quiet down, open up, and you hear the word "Wait." This can be one of the hardest things to trust and follow. You probably have been taught good things only come with hard work. Most of the time, waiting can seem like the "wrong" thing to do. You may try to paddle awhile and find that you get nowhere. Then you wait as long as you can stand it and go back to paddling some more. All kinds of things can come up here. Frustration and doubt are just a couple of the possibilities. Sometimes we are told to sit tight and wait. For the full power of the universe to come together, you may need to wait for several factors to line up at the same time. This situation can also be a time to rest for what is to come. You may have been heading to an island that didn't yet have a dock built to receive you. Timing can be everything in our lives. The universe doesn't always work on our time table! ☺ When it is time, the wind will come back and off you go again!

Always stay open to stepping back and looking at your goals from all angles. Periodically, ask yourself again, "What do I want? I used to want this, but what do I want now?" Look at all you have learned so far and appreciate the journey. You may decide that it's time for a new goal. The previous goal may have been just a way to get you started so you could uncover what you needed to uncover.

Just setting a goal can lead to growth. To begin with, identifying a goal can lead you to question whether you feel you deserve to achieve that goal. Whether your goal is about happiness or success, having love in your life or increasing your abilities, parts of you believe fully that you should be able to obtain the goal and parts doubt that very same thing. We all have parts of us that believe in scarcity, that believe lies we've been told like the one that there's only a certain amount of love to go around in the world. We all have parts of us that that believe to have success, happiness, or any amount of achievement, you have to work really hard and only a few people deserve it. Most of us have the lie inside of us that we are not good enough. These are the obstructions that try to keep you from allowing abundance in your life fully and allowing your greatness to come through.

It can be a very healing experience all in itself just to write specific goals for what you want to draw towards your life, what you want to achieve. The process of writing your goals can also bring you face to face with the fears and lies limiting your growth and healing. The more specific the goal, the more powerful it can be. The goal needs to be clear, something you can see and measure, something functional.

A vague goal is a stumbling block to growth. Here are some examples of vague goals: I want to be happy: I want to have more peace; I want to be all that I can be. If your goal is vague, you won't be able to see your progress. If your goal is too vague, it really can't be obtained. You can always want more happiness and peace. These vague goals set you up to reinforce your failures. How will you know when you are all you can be? Being all you can be is a lifelong goal, so how do you look back and determine you are more today than you were yesterday? If you have vague goals, how will you be able to see the areas in which you have grown and expanded and the areas that still need more focus?

To create really powerful goals, state where you are right now and then declare some small, short-term goals and some bigger, long-term goals. As time passes, when you look back to get a sense of your progress, this approach to setting goals helps you recall your starting point and see the increments of progress you have made. Make your goal statements specific. Often, as time passes, you make more change than you are willing to credit yourself for making. Stating your goals with specificity gives you the opportunity to focus on how much you have improved rather than on how far you still have to go. If you don't begin with a specific starting point, it's hard to see how far you have gone.

For example, if your goal is to bring more peace into your life, first state some specific situations in which you get caught up in the chaos. One of these might be that during your morning commute you get frustrated and you notice your shoulders are tense and angry when you get to work. Now go into even more detail. As you drive into work, you notice within 5 minutes that you start getting tense and irritated, within 30 minutes that you are angry, your jaw is clamped, and your shoulders feel like rocks. At about 35 minutes into the drive, if someone cuts you off, you honk your horn and yell at them. At about that same time in your drive, you notice you start getting upset whenever you have to stop at a red light, drumming on the steering wheel and muttering. Stating specific details about your starting point will make it easier to form some goals.

It's also extremely important to state goals specifically and positively. As you do so, notice it can be difficult to state a goal in a positive way. Usually, you state what you don't want instead of what you do want. For instance, you might first state a short term goal as "I want to drive 30 minutes without anger and without tension in my shoulders." When you state your goal like this, you're making your goal be about something you don't want—anger and tension in your muscles—instead of what you do want—calm emotions and soft muscles. A short-term goal could be as simple as "I want to remain peaceful and have my muscles remain at ease for 15 minutes during my morning commute." This is a very specific, positive, functional goal and one clear enough that you can use it to make a meaningful assessment when you review your progress.

With a clearly stated goal like this one, you make it possible to notice that you could only make the goal for 5 minutes in the beginning, but now you can make it for 20 minutes. Without this kind of clear, short-term goal, you might think back on the past six months and notice that you still can't make it all the way to work while remaining peaceful and at ease; with this assessment, you may feel like a failure. By setting specific goals and then reviewing them, you can look back and see how much you have changed. For instance, a specific goal would enable you to notice that when people cut you off, while you used to get so angry you would honk and yell at them, now you rarely do that. A clear and specific goal also gives you the opportunity to see what needs more focus. For instance, you may find that your shoulders still get tense quickly. You may need to see what else you can do to help with this. Perhaps your shoulders need some treatment. Maybe you need to adjust your car seat. Having the specifics written down gives you a point of comparison so you can see the areas you have improved and the ones still needing your focus.

Now, we will look at setting a goal that has to do with relieving pain. When my patients set a goal based on relieving pain, they can have a difficult time stating it in a positive way. Suppose you have knee pain. When I ask you for a goal, you may have a tendency to state something like, "I want to be able to walk without pain." This goal focuses entirely on what you *don't* want: pain. When I ask people to change the goal to state what they *do* want, they often have a hard time finding the words. Their focus has always been on stopping the pain and they are literally unable to think of how they could describe walking without the word "pain" in it. The pain is so encompassing they can't see around it.

I coach them a little, asking, "What would you like to be able to walk like?" They may still answer, "Without pain." So then I'll ask what walking like that would look like. What is walking without pain? What would you call that? Sometimes it's very difficult for someone to come up with words like ease, grace, or fluidity, because pain has been such a part of their life for so long they've forgotten the other side of it.

An example of a positive end goal is "I would like to walk 30 minutes with ease." That can seem like a very small change but it can make all the difference in the world. Many times it will be like a light bulb goes on, and the client says, "Yes! That's what I want!" Once the words change from what they don't want to what they do want, their focus changes, and they can make progress. Now they can start to visualize what they want: walking smoothly, confidently, with ease, or whatever other focus they choose. Whatever you focus on is what you'll bring into your life, so you want to focus on what you want to do and achieve, rather than on what you don't want to do. If you're focusing on getting rid of pain, then the focus is on pain and that's what will keep coming. If you change your focus to ease, grace, and fluidity, then you're opening yourself up to the possibility of achieving those experiences.

As with every goal, when setting a goal of relieving pain, first state where you are right now in as much detail as possible. It might be something like, "When I walk, I feel a tension in my right knee, and within 5 minutes I start to have a burning pain that goes up into the right side of my back. At 10 minutes, the pain starts to become throbbing and sharp, and after 15 minutes I need to stop." You might also say of your current situation something like, "When I walk, I keep my arms stiff and at my sides. My shoulders feel braced, and I feel tension in my neck."

Remember your entire body is connected, so your goals should involve your entire body, not just the symptom areas. Really pay attention to everything you feel in your body. Don't just focus on the one place that has pain; expand your focus to include your entire body. What do your feet feel like when you walk? What do your thighs feel like, your calves? How about your neck? What are your hands doing? Expand outward because you'll start to notice there is more going on than your awareness even recognized. The more detail you have, the more you can notice as you improve.

A short-term goal might be that you would like to be able to walk 10 minutes with equal stride lengths and with fluidity in your hips. Another short-term goal could be to walk for 10 minutes with your shoulders being soft, your arms swinging, and your neck at ease. A long-term goal could be to do the same for 30-45 minutes.

If a month goes by and you still have some pain, you might get frustrated. This is a good time to pull out the goals and see what has or hasn't changed. As you read and are reminded of your starting point, you may become aware you still have pain in your back after 10 minutes, but now your legs feel softer and more relaxed, your neck is at ease, and your arms and shoulders are swinging. By re-reading your goal statements, especially the details of your starting point, you can see that even though you still have the knee pain, things are progressing and you are moving forward. The more detail you can put into these goals and into the description of your starting point, the more you can see your changes. Sometimes your main symptom will be the last piece to go. You might have to unlock everything else before your back can move with ease. That's why it's very important to state both short- and long-term goals, and to make sure they are functional. State goals in terms of what you can see or measure. Document in detail your starting point so that you can see the progress.

Goals are meant to help you see how far you have progressed. They act as guideposts to help you evaluate your next step. Do not look at goals as a way to see what you haven't accomplished. If you state and work with goals in the correct way, they actually help inspire you to see the subtle changes happening as you move along and help you move forward more easily. Always remember goals are meant to be dynamic and you will probably change them as you go.

Let's return to the earlier walking goal to use as an example of how a goal needs to be dynamic and able to change. Suppose that when you stop to re-evaluate your progress, you recall you originally felt most of your pain in your right knee, but you notice now your left hip has gotten tighter. In this case, you may want to change some of your goals and treatments to focus on the left hip.

The same is true with any goal. As you progress toward a goal, you will notice that as you improve in one area, another area comes up needing to have some focus. Once you set your original course (goal), your life will evolve to help guide you to places you didn't even know were possible to reach when you first started out. So remember to be dynamic and flexible with your goals.

## We are Co-creators

I want to address an important idea here: the belief that we can create anything we want. The truth is each of us is a co-creator in his or her life. Making and setting goals is a way to open yourself to your fullest potential. It aligns you to receive assistance from the universe and helps you open up to the abundance in this world. There is a difference between this concept and the mentality that we can create anything we want or that we can manifest anything we want to in our life. Co-creation does not imply that if you just think positively enough and put up pictures of what you want, you will get whatever you want. That mentality falls right back into the idea that "If I am good, I will get rewarded."

We are not the creators of this universe, but we are co-creators. We are much more powerful than we ever knew, and that's the whole thing with these goals. Every thought and every word is powerful and creative; each is a force. By focusing on what we *do* want, we then open ourselves up to the possibility of that happening. Let me repeat: we open ourselves up to the *possibility* of something happening or of manifesting what we want into our lives. The sticking point is that what we think we want may not be what we need in order to reach our full spiritual potential. We don't know what our full purpose is in this life; that is something revealed to us, not something we can create. We don't know what full lessons we were meant to learn, in what ways we are to grow in this life. We may not be meant to drive a Mercedes.

The error of believing that somehow wanting something the "right way" will get you whatever you want in life is stimulated by books like *The Secret*. People read a book like that and think that if they just follow a certain formula, they will get everything they want. Their focus is on material things instead of where it is meant to be: enhancing spiritual life. People fall into the ego trap and think that if they just put pictures up on a board and think every day about whatever it is they desire, they are going to get all these *things*: the perfect house, the perfect spouse, the perfect job, the perfect car, the perfect location in the world to live, retire by 20 years old and be on a yacht.

It is good to ask for what you want and to open yourself up to receive these things, but what if your desire doesn't manifest? Does that mean you did something wrong? Do you blame yourself that you're not on a yacht but instead driving a beat up old car? This way of thinking causes us to put pressure on ourselves and to blame ourselves if we don't get what we want. The truth is that we don't know what is in our best interest. Perhaps to learn the full value of abundance you must first experience scarcity. What if abundance has nothing to do with money? What if learning about abundance is realizing the simple things are what matter, that every breath you take is sacred and special.

We are here for spiritual development and growth, but our ego likes to make us think we are here to acquire physical "things." Unfortunately, most of us in the Western cultures tend to equate happiness with more and bigger. The more you have and the bigger it is, the happier you must be. But all of that is empty. What truly matters is what is within the soul.

I see people struggling all the time because they understand books like *The Secret* to mean they can create happiness by wanting things, instead of understanding it's about opening up to abundance and receiving. We often and erroneously equate "abundance and receiving" to mean "getting things." Misreading the meaning of these books, many people believe they have the power to create anything in this world; they just need to think it and it will happen. There is nothing wrong with having abundance in the form of wealth or material things, as long as it's not your final goal, because those things are not going to make you happy. The meaning in a book like *The Secret* is that there is *always* abundance, no matter what your situation. Obtaining material things is not what this is about; it's about growing and expanding, and feeling gratitude for everything you have in your life.

Setting goals and asking for what you want is the way to open yourself up to the possibility of all your dreams. Asking for more love in your life, wanting to be at peace with your financial situation, picturing a new house or car... these wants are fine goals to establish. The problem comes when we fall into the "I will be happy when I have this or own that" mentality, into the belief that having "more stuff" leads to happiness. This is the very reason so many people have financial woes right now. They fell into the trap of buying "stuff" they couldn't afford because they thought if they just had more, they would be happy. Frequently, our challenges, or the things that we often consider to be bad, actually help to open us by revealing a gift or talent we didn't even know was there. I am sure you have heard stories of someone losing a job and, because of it, finally venturing off into the career they had always desired but hadn't pursued. When we ask but do not receive, it may be because we are meant to head down another road.

Co-creation is about doing your part: visualizing what you want, working to achieve what you visualize, and being open to change your course if what you want isn't what you are supposed to have. You may need a sickness or an injury, or you may need to lose your job, in order to cultivate a talent inside of yourself and get stronger so you can go in a direction you had no idea you were going to go. We need to stop looking at wanting a new car, a new house, or a promotion as a way to define spiritual growth, and stop seeing the acquisition of such things as validation that we have obtained spiritual growth. Spiritual growth has nothing to do with amassing money, fancy objects, or cars. Obtaining these things does not indicate you have grown spiritually.

If you are on the path that's meant for you, you might have riches and abundance sometimes; other times, your path may be in staying simple. Perhaps you are supposed to learn how to appreciate the simple things in life, so you may not have what the world would consider abundant riches, but you may feel more satisfied than those who have vast material wealth. We have to keep in mind we are not God and, no matter how much we try, we cannot control life. We can open ourselves up to let our path be as easy as possible, to let in the things we would like. Then we need to realize God will provide us with what we need, not always what we want.

## What are you really asking for?

When you ask for something, what are you really asking for? What you think you are asking to come into your life, and what actually comes into your life, often can be completely different things. For example, if your stated goal is "I want to have more peace in my life" you might picture asking for this is going to bring sunny days filled with hours of basking in a field enjoying the tranquil peace and quiet. But, you may notice in the days, weeks, and months following this request, you are actually getting the opposite. You find your life filled with more chaos then ever! What did you do wrong? Nothing! You just had an expectation that was different from what really happens. When you say, "I want more peace in my life" what you are really saying is, "Please help me to be able to connect to peace even in chaos." Having internal peace means you can be in chaos without it affecting you. So, when you ask for more peace, life will keep giving you chaos until you can find your peace inside of the chaos.

Another example of how your stated goal might mean something other than what you have in mind is the goal "I want to feel more love in my life." Often, you make this goal when you feel you lack love in your life. So, to help you feel more love, life will put you in situations that bring up your fears around love, the kinds of situations that usually cause you to close yourself off from the love that is always there. This will keep happening until you finally realize love is always there, just like air is always there; you just have to open up and receive it.

## The "Yeah... but"

When you are creating goals or setting your intentions, be aware of the "yeah... but." Here are some examples of the "yeah... but." "Yeah, I would really like to have that but..." "Yeah, I would really like to go there but..." "Yeah, I would like to do this but..." "... but I can't because

I'd lose my secure job" "… but I can't because I'd upset everyone." The "Yeah… but" shows up when anyone tries to suggest you change your life in any way and your first response is "Yeah… but" and you go on to list all the reasons why you can't reach your goal, why you can't change your life.

"Yeah… but" is how you explain or justify why you can't have what you think you need. It's a way to try to blame somebody or something outside of you for your inability or unwillingness to progress toward a goal or dream. Whenever this sort of justification comes up, take time to stop and go into these reasons, as these are the fears keeping you from doing your part in the co-creation. There are always a million reasons why you can't do what you want to do, but if you are truly being told to do it, then you need to take responsibility for your part of the deal and do your work. Sure it will be scary. Change is scary. But to not do it will literally keep you from living.

## Summary and final thoughts on goals

Here are some key points about goals:

- Make sure your goals are things you can actually see and visualize.

- Make goals as functional as possible so you can tell when a change has occurred.

- Make sure your goals are stated in the positive way.

- Write both short- and long-term goals.

- Describe your starting point in detail.

- Be open to really putting out there everything you want.

- Let it be fun and let go of any limits.

Here are some great questions to ask when setting goals:

- Who would I be if I didn't know who I couldn't be?

- What could I do if I didn't know what I couldn't do?

- Who would I be without the fears that hold me back?

Consider all kinds of fear here, for example: fear of making mistakes, being made a fool, being successful. Take time to go over this carefully, to look at all the limiting beliefs preventing you from succeeding. It's time to bring in all the power we have in the process of co-creation.

It is a great idea to write down your goals and then have other people look over them for you. You may be surprised at how often you will focus on the negative and not even notice! Having someone else go over your goals can help you see ways in which you're not even consciously aware that you're limiting yourself and your growth.

Remember to let go of the mindset that seemingly negative occurrences such as a car accident, a house fire, or the loss of your job, are the result of your doing something wrong. Stop believing the lie that if you had just thought positively enough, had burned enough candles, or said the right prayers, you would've gotten everything you sought. Stop making obtaining material objects the reward for living a spiritual life. The real reward for leading a truly spiritual life is that you can see every aspect of your life as it is meant to be, even when it's different from what you think it should be. This is the balance between asking for what you want and then letting go of the outcome. It can be very difficult to understand this concept, especially for people in the western world. Can you be open to believe you have done everything you are supposed to do and you are on your spiritual path, even if you lose it all? That is the real test. When you reach the point that you truly know you are always on your path—in abundance, and in scarcity and loss—then you can truly detach from the outcome and you will be free to fully receive without limits.

## Chapter 21

*Detaching from the Outcome*

Detaching from the outcome of the goals you have set can seem like a very confusing idea. After all, we are taught that once we have a goal, we are supposed to work and force and push and fight until we make that goal occur. Let's look at the sailboat analogy again to help with understanding the concepts of detaching from the outcome and co-creating.

When you intend to sail, you may have a course mapped out that you really think you are supposed to travel. Suppose you set your sails but then there's no wind. What does that mean? It could mean a lot of different things. As I discussed earlier, it might mean that it's time to wait, that it's a test of patience. You are asked to trust that the wind will come. Or, it might mean you need to start paddling, you need to work for a while on your own before the wind comes to get you going there.

How do you know what to do? You try things. If you start paddling and all of a sudden the wind and waves come up, and they push you in the opposite direction, then that may be telling you to wait. If you aren't sure and you continue to fight and the wind keeps blowing, then at some point you will need to stop and re-evaluate.

If you detach from the outcome, then you can be open to listen to guidance when it says it is time to change directions or wait. Detaching from the outcome, you will be able to let go of how you think it should be and trust that you will be guided. Can you trust you will get what you need, even if it's not always what you want or think it should be? If you are not able to detach from the outcome, you may find you continue to exhaust yourself trying to go in a direction you aren't supposed to go.

Your part of co-creation is to go through the steps, setting clear and detailed goals, visualizing them, clearing all your fears and blocks, and being open to be guided to the work you need to do to progress toward your goals. Then, you let go of the idea that the goal has to be achieved or is the way you *must* go. You do your part and you let go of the outcome.

Returning to the sailboat analogy, letting go does not mean you just sit back in your lounge chair, have a cold drink, and wait for your goal to come to you. No, you will have to do your work. You will need to adjust the sails as the wind shifts, keep the boat maintained, keep watch on the horizon for storms or other trouble, etc. You'll need to work; at times it may be very hard, and at times it may seem like it is easy. Sometimes everything will just flow. The sky is clear and the wind is blowing in the direction you want to go. At those times you can sit back and enjoy yourself while staying open to guidance.

It is important to stay open at all times to noticing the signs and guidance around you. If you are open to the signs, you will know when a storm is coming and you will have time to put your sails down and prepare the boat. It may mean you get taken off course, but the signs are clear. If you ignore the signs or think you shouldn't put your sails down because you want to get to your destination, the storm may swamp your boat or tear the sails. There may be times when you will need to bail out the water as the storm rages, and these times can seem to last forever. These times may be necessary to test your resolve in pursuing your set course.

Remember there is a difference between doing your part and fighting against what is supposed to be. There is a difference between fighting the guidance you are given and working to keep yourself on course during the storms of life. Storms will occur. Surviving the storm and fighting against the storm are two different things. If you choose to fight the storm, you will finally exhaust yourself and then you will be taken where you are supposed to go anyway. If you choose fighting the storm, your boat may be destroyed in the battle. Surviving the storm may mean going with the direction of the wind (even if it's the "wrong" way) to keep your boat in one piece.

You need to find the balance between doing your part and staying open to seeing the signs of where you're supposed to go; this way, you're always working with nature (the divine). You want to be connected with and work with the divine, whether you call it God, Buddha, energy, or something else. It will work the same regardless of the name you call it.

Trusting the process can be one of the hardest things you will be asked to do. This trust is particularly hard to extend when you are not going in a direction you want to go. What if you're asked to just wait? Can you do that? We're so trained to the idea that pursuing goals demands constant motion and action. What will you do if your guidance suggests to you that you're just supposed to wait for a while?

I like to use the following analogy to help with understanding the concept of trusting the process. Suppose you want to move a car up a hill, but you don't have the keys. This might be a time to wait. You can try to push a car up a hill all day, all week, all year, but all you're going to be doing is wasting a lot of energy. If you are given the signal to wait, then wait. When the person comes with the keys to the car, then you can get in and drive the car up the hill. You still make it to the top of the hill; you will just be using a lot less effort.

When it's time for action to happen, it will happen. When it's time for you to rest, make sure you take that rest. Rest doesn't mean you don't do anything actively, because you are always looking for the signs. Sometimes you just need a time to rest, recover, and reconnect with yourself fully. Sometimes there's some pretty big stuff ahead for you to do soon and you need to be fully refreshed.

The only way to learn how to connect and trust your guidance is to try it. Listen for guidance. If you aren't sure of your guidance, try one of your options. You may sometimes force when you are supposed to rest and sometimes rest when you are supposed to be acting. These aren't mistakes in such cases. These are times when you are learning how to listen to guidance. You can't learn to recognize how you're being guided by observing; you do it by living.

Remember, detaching isn't choosing to be passive. Detaching is an active process of opening, listening, and trusting, and it takes practice. As you practice, it will become easier for you to hear and act upon the guidance you are given. Doing this leads you to put your energy into the process in the most efficient manner, where you can combine your energy with the energy of the divine force. This is how you can move a mountain with a mustard seed.

Chapter 22

*Chaos is Clarity*

How many times do we ask for clarity? If we only knew where, what, when, and why, then it would be "okay." If only we could buy the *Cliff Notes* for our life. Why can't we have an $a + b = c$ answer? We are taught there is a logical and linear approach to life (oh, but that isn't true, is it?), so there must be a way to have a linear and logical approach to our healing journey or our growth process. Right?

This linear and logical approach does seem to underlie the philosophy behind some branches of meditation, yoga, and breathing practice, as well as some seminars and books on creation and various forms of inner-work. We're told that if we just follow a formula of thought, breathing, or bodywork, or if we assemble the right combination of crystals, candles, and oils, we will be able to obtain a state of perpetual peace, clarity, and calmness. This mindset traps us again in the belief that if you just do it "right," you will be rewarded. It also implies we can obtain a state where there will never be chaos and where we will always be "happy."

First, I want to look how we can be trapped by the belief that if we grow or we reach a certain point in our spiritual growth, we will be happy all the time. If happiness is your goal in your growth process, you may want to re-evaluate what you are doing. Growing and becoming more spiritual means opening up to living in a way aligned with what your spirit wants. The spiritual wants and needs are not the same as worldly or physical needs. The spirit needs to live in ways that bring passion and love to its life. I am not speaking of the worldly beliefs of conditional love and temporary passion. This is about living in a way that feels true to your spirit, even if it does not follow the rules and wants of the human world.

Happiness occurs when you stop trying to make yourself happy through physical means and start allowing your spirit or soul to guide you. I came to a deeper understanding about the pursuit of happiness when reading *Dancing with Life*, by Phillip Moffitt. In his book, Moffitt talks about the Buddhist concept that suffering is a part of living. Some people take that to mean life is about suffering, but that's not the case. The secret to being content or "happy" is in knowing there will be suffering or times when you are uncomfortable. It's about accepting there will be times of joy and times of sadness. There will be times when the sun shines and times when it rains. When you stop believing one of these shouldn't happen, you will stop needless pain.

I prefer to use the word "unease" where others refer to "suffering" because of how I define suffering. To me, suffering comes from resisting what is. I believe suffering is a choice, whereas being uneasy or uncomfortable at times in life is a given, like the rain.

I also liked the descriptions of different types of suffering in Moffitt's *Dancing with Life*. These descriptions helped me come to understand the constant, low-level unease I felt, even at moments when I felt truly happy and content. What follows now is a very limited and condensed version of what I got from reading *Dancing with Life*. If what you read here seems to speak to you, I encourage you to read the book, as it is full of great insights.

Moffitt talked about different levels of unease. Some of the unease we feel is at a level we can change; it is in our control. This level of unease is what I call suffering; it's the pain we choose to take on when we resist what is happening in our life. We suffer when we fight what is happening in our lives; for example, when we blame others, when we have lost someone or something we love, when we believe we are separate from love.

Another level of unease is the type we feel because our physical form knows it's time is limited. Our physical bodies will eventually die. This causes a general unease and sometimes a feeling of unsettledness. There is also a level of unease stemming from the fact we are spiritual beings in physical bodies; a part of our spirit will never feel at ease until it returns home, returns to the spiritual realm.

This book helped me understand a concept that I had had difficulty feeling as truth. I had been told so many times that if I was not content, there must be something "wrong." If I was not content, I was told something in my life needed to change, either externally or internally. Moffitt's perspective opened me up to the idea that no matter how perfectly things were going, there might be a part of my spirit that is always uneasy because it longs to be home, or a part of my physical body that is always uneasy because it knows it's time is limited.

None of this means you can't be happy and content while you are here on Earth. Instead, it frees you from expecting you *should* be happy and content. If you think you *should* be happy, when you aren't happy, you think you need to change. If instead you can just open yourself up to the possibility there will always be a little bit of unease and let go of the need to try to change it, you stop fighting the unease and in turn become more content. By realizing my being uneasy was just as normal an occurrence as the rain, instead of thinking it needed to be changed, I was able to become more content. Being more content produced the side-effect of being happy. Happiness occurs when you stop trying to change things in your life in the hope you will be happy.

Now let's look at another idea that gets in the way of growth. This is the idea that if you do it right, things will be clear and there will no longer be chaos in your life. Just observe nature and you will see the problem with setting a goal like this. The life cycles fluctuate between calm and chaos. There are moments of calm and moments of chaos, such as storms, floods, droughts, earthquakes. There are times when nature has to strip away all the excess to bring about change or new growth. The same rules apply to our lives too. We have to be stripped clean, freed of everything holding us back, so new growth can occur.

Nature demonstrates that cycle perfectly. Consider the cycles of the seasons in the northern part of the United States. When winter comes, all the leaves are stripped from the trees. The trees are naked and exposed throughout the winter. If you walk through the woods at that time, you might think the trees are dead. Then, spring comes and with it the new buds and new life. The leaves and flowers spring out of the earth and the trees. Now everywhere are the brilliant, lush colors of the various leaves, grasses, and spring plants, and a beautiful display of all the spring flowers. Throughout summer there is an ever-changing display of flowers and of the leaves on the trees. When fall arrives, it's an amazing season of changing masterpieces each day, as the leaves turn vibrant shades of yellow, red, orange, brown, and a mix of them all. After the life has left the leaves and flowers, they then let go and return to the earth to help fertilize next year's growth. That is one of the cycles of life. This cycle will continue.

The same kind of cycle will occur with each of us throughout our lifetime. We will be stripped continually of everything we think we know so new growth can occur. No matter how much we advance in our spiritual growth, this cycle will not stop. If we believe chaos is wrong or shouldn't happen, we will never be able to mature fully in our spiritual growth. Fighting change would be like running around madly in the fall, trying to tape the leaves back on the trees because you don't want winter to come, don't want that phase in your life. If you realize the cycles will always continue, it will help you appreciate fully each cycle instead of trying to stop the cycle in just the "on" phase. Instead of dreading winter, you can embrace this phase as the time of opening and resting.

There are the normal cycles of life—like the cycle of the sun setting and rising—and there are also the cycles of disasters. We also have the regular cycles of life and also cycles of what we consider disasters. In nature there are tidal waves, volcanoes, and forest fires. These can cause such destruction that when they occur, it may seem at the time like nothing good could ever happen. In natural disasters like these, it seems like things have been changed forever and usually things have indeed changed forever. If you have ever watched coverage of an area stricken by natural disaster, you have probably also seen that such disasters create amazing opportunities for people to reach out and to heal. In natural disasters, peoples' lives are changed forever and take directions they never would have imagined. Natural disaster also creates an opportunity for nature to change and for new growth to occur. For example, some seeds are only released during fires. In such cases, the fire destroys parts of the forest but also releases these seeds and new growth occurs.

You don't have to have chaos for growth to occur. Growth can also occur in times of calm. For our own growth, we need to remember cycles of chaos and calm will continue to occur, and so we should stop fighting against the chaos thinking that it shouldn't occur. This is the goal of spiritual growth: being able to feel peace in the midst of chaos. Remembering that "This too shall pass" can help with coming to a place of balance and peace. No matter where you are in the cycle—in the calm or in the chaos—this too shall pass. You can take comfort in this understanding when you are hurting, as you know it will pass. Similarly, understanding this can help you appreciate feeling joy, as it will also pass. Clarity comes when you know chaos is truly a part of life, a part of the cycle. Then you can embrace each phase of the cycle and find that the place of peace and stability is within *you*.

Section 5

# Returning to Our True Self

Chapter 23

*We are That which We Seek*

As you progress on your journey, keep in mind you are already what you seek. This journey is about revealing the masterpiece that is already there, not about changing how you are or becoming something you aren't. Michelangelo made a statement about this principle that has been used in many of the seminars I have attended and in many of the books I have read. When asked how he got the inspiration to create his statues, Michelangelo responded that those masterpieces were already within the stone and that his job was just to reveal the beauty by chipping away the excess stone. Our journey of returning to our true self is just the same: chipping away at the things preventing our beauty from shining through. There's no question of whether we are brilliant or deserve to be great; we are already. Each one of us is created in the image of the master designer, called God by some and different names by others. The truth is that the brilliance of the divine is within each and every one of us. We are full of beauty and we are full of grace. We *are* beauty and we *are* grace.

In the first section of this book, I discussed the various ways we lose ourselves. Those ways of losing ourselves—the traumas occurring in our lives, the false beliefs and lies we take on, the masks we wear—all become the things we need to chip away to reveal the brilliance of our spirit and soul. Each and every one of us is like a beautiful stained glass window that has had a buildup of film. This film is from the judgments, lies, and traumas that have been part of our lives. The film develops in times we took on lies like "I am not good enough" or "I don't deserve to be loved." Our healing journey involves clearing this film so our amazing beauty can shine through fully. The truth of this beauty applies to everyone. Thinking that we are better than, or less than, anyone else puts more film on us and separates us from our true essence. We are all from the same source and we are all connected no matter what our hair color, skin color, sex, ethnic background, birthplace, or any other of our physical or circumstantial characteristics.

Along your journey, you will reach points at which you feel you can't continue. For example, at some point you may connect to a place where all you can feel is ugliness within yourself, where you may have uncovered some self-hate. When you reach points like these, it's a good time to surround yourself with beauty. Go to a park, visit some of your favorite friends, watch a sunset. While surrounding yourself with beauty in some way, remember you can only see in others what you see in yourself. So, as you look on something beautiful, whether it's a person or a sunset, remind yourself that the beauty you see is a reflection of your true self.

The journey to your true self is more like a returning home than a trek to find beauty or love outside of yourself. It's a process of chipping away, of remembering we are an amazing, vibrant essence full of beauty inside and out. The journey to our true self is truly about the realization that we are already all we are seeking. To reconnect to your true self, you need to start to detach from the lies or the false self.

## Chapter 24

# *Detaching from the False Self*

How do we go about this process of starting to determine what comes from our false self and what from our true self? The Bible provides a good insight here: "The truth shall set you free." This same philosophy is found in virtually every spiritual text. The path of discovery, of healing, starts with uncovering what is really our truth and what is really not our truth. The process is also about becoming aware of all the lies we tell ourselves and others. Each person needs to come to his own truths through feeling and with openness, looking at his thoughts and the true intentions behind each of his actions. Are you acting from your truth or are you reacting from the programming? By taking this approach, you can start to see what is really driving you, what is in control of you.

To start, you need to understand, as I discussed earlier in this book, you are being driven by your programmed beliefs and judgments. It's like having multiple personalities within you. These beliefs and personalities influence every decision you make and every action you take. Books that go into detail about just this idea alone have names for the different personalities. I will give a few of the many examples available. One of the personalities is sometimes called the prostitute, the personality that causes you to sell yourself. This is the personality in control when, for example, you stay in a marriage because you are afraid of not being able to make it on your own financially, or you stay in a job you hate because it pays well. These are examples of selling a piece of yourself. What is the cost to you? Can you think of some areas in your life in which the prostitute has control?

Another example of a personality that might be within you is the victim. When this personality comes out, it uses any drama to its advantage. "You can't blame me for my actions because I was abused as a child." This is the personality that likes to make you believe you are justified in acting a particular way or in getting some kind of benefits because you have a hardship or trauma in your history. The hero is another of these personalities. This is the part that drives you to try to "save the world," to go from one cause to the next, whether it be saving the stray dogs or the abused children. This is not to say that we shouldn't try to improve the world around us; however, this personality keeps you jumping from one cause to the next so that you keep your energy focused outside of yourself.

These are just three examples of personalities. Carolyn Myss writes about these different personalities in depth in her books; they are also discussed in many other books. To help progress to reaching your true self, you just need to start to become aware of the intent behind your actions. Did you act a certain way because you were moved to do so by your spirit, or were you moved by your hero or victim personality?

The fear of scarcity is another significant consideration, as it can cause you to make decisions against your true spirit. Do you believe in scarcity or abundance? If you are driven by the fear of scarcity, you believe there is not enough—not enough money, love, food, or anything else—for everyone to be content. In every situation in life, you are driven by a fear that if you don't act quickly or make the right decision, there won't be enough for you. You believe there is not enough love for everyone, so you withhold your love, loving only certain people in your life. You also believe there will never be enough love for you.

Believing in scarcity, you believe there's not enough money for everyone, so you hoard your money and worry constantly that you could lose what money you have at any time. Your thoughts are consumed with ways you can make more money or insure your money is safe. If you believe in scarcity, it doesn't matter if you have a mansion, three cars, and millions of dollars in the bank; you are still consumed with a fear of losing it all. This is a very fear driven mindset. People who believe in scarcity are easily swayed to believe others ought to be feared because those others might come and take what they have. Another trait of those who believe in scarcity is no matter how much they have, they always desire more. They have little appreciation or gratitude for what they do have because scarcity makes them feel they are always lacking something.

How would it be different if you believed in abundance? If you have the mindset of abundance, you believe there is more than enough for everyone. You are open to giving freely because you know the more you give, the more you receive. You aren't controlled by the fear of scarcity. You aren't consumed by the need to own material objects, because you are content with the simple things in life. You aren't controlled by the mindset that you don't have enough, because you truly believe you already have what you need. And, if there is something else you want, you know it will make its way to you if you truly need it, because there is an abundance of all things.

If you believe in abundance, you will be full of gratitude and appreciation for everything you have in your life. You love freely and openly because you believe if someone you love leaves your life, there are many who will come to fill that spot. You know there is an abundance of people for you to love and by whom you can be loved. Believing in abundance is believing in the flow of life, believing things flow in and out in a constant cycle. The only time the flow stops is if you block it with fears of scarcity and with hoarding. Believing in abundance helps you because things just seem to come your way when you need them.

There are people who say they believe in abundance, but who actually are driven by the fear of scarcity. These are the people who throw their money away saying they believe in abundance and know there is always going to be enough, but they really are scared and acting out of their fear. These people spend their money foolishly instead of giving when they are guided by their spirit. When you act out of fear in your giving, it is the same as hoarding and leads to a block in the flow. In every aspect of your life and in finding your balance, you do best when you allow yourself to be guided by your spirit instead of acting out of fear.

As I mentioned, there are books that go into more complete detail about the various personalities and how they can be influencing your life. I am bringing up some examples here to give you an idea of this concept. I encourage you to explore this subject more thoroughly by seeing which books attract you, as doing so will definitely be beneficial on your journey of growth. Each one of these personalities is within you, some more predominant than others. As you understand the pitfalls of these personalities, you can start to break free and begin to act and live from your true spirit.

Which of the personalities become more predominant in you depends on what you learn from your family, close friends, and community. If you were raised in a family that is very fearful of not having enough money, that same fear will likely be passed on to you. If you were raised in a family whose members are very open and compassionate to each other, that abundance of love will usually be passed on to you. If you come from a very stoic family that does not show love, or one that shows love only briefly and then only at the times when you've done something they deemed deserving of love, you will probably take on these same traits and have the mindset that there is a scarcity of love. This kind of upbringing generally passes on the belief love is a precious commodity that should only be given in very small doses at any given time and only when the receiver has done something to "deserve" the love and praise. You will benefit from taking the time to find the books or seminars that reach out to you so you have help uncovering any beliefs, fears, and personalities that may be controlling you.

As I discussed earlier in the trigger chapter, most of your day-to-day decisions are actually reactions based on what you were taught in the past—that is, based on your programming—and you rarely act based truly and solely on the current situation. Your actions in the present are primarily reactions based on reactions to similar situations in the past. Your perception of your current situation is shadowed by your past experiences. To connect to your true self totally means to live fully in the current moment, and that means being *present*. If you want to start becoming more present, you need to start to differentiate between the many voices in your head. You need to determine which one of these voices is from the true self and which ones are based in fear and past perceptions. You can use the same process for uncovering the true and false voices as you use to uncover the core of triggers. When you feel yourself reacting with anger or fear, instead of saying, "I'm afraid" or "I'm angry" and wondering why you feel the way you do, start to detach from your reaction. You may find using statements like "There is anger inside of me" or "There is fear inside of me" will enable you to detach from the reaction and to step into your present feelings instead. Taking this approach allows you to determine if you are re-acting or actually feeling an appropriate response to the present situation.

Remember, this isn't about trying to control your feelings or about not feeling at all. Emotions from joy to rage are meant to be felt fully and deeply. Emotions aren't good or bad; they are sensations meant to help guide you. On your journey to uncovering your true self, you will find that you feel more deeply than you have in your life because you are being moved by your current situation. You will feel the emotions more deeply and feel them more connected to your soul. This process is about learning to discern when you are acting and feeling what is true to your current situation and when you are reacting. Being present is freedom. Reacting is being caught in a prison with walls and bars formed by lies and hurts you carry from your past.

When you find yourself caught in a reaction, your false self (ego) will encourage you to strike out at others, to blame others, to go into victim mentality, and to want to try to manipulate others. Unfortunately, many of us have been taught these ways of reacting. This is especially true in our society, where we have the mindset that if anything goes "wrong," someone else needs to be blamed. Whenever something "wrong" happens, it's not our fault. This will cause you to go straight to your self-made prison. To break free, you need to stop looking outside, stop blaming others, and see what is there for you to learn and heal.

Eckhart Tolle's book *A New Earth* is a very good reference on how to recognize the ways ego tries to manipulate you and keep you out of the present. It is a great source of information on breaking free from the various controlling voices inside your head and becoming more present. As you start the process of freeing yourself from the voices in your head, you give attention to those voices and learn to differentiate them. One voice may be full of anxiety; another may always have an angry tone; while another always brings up all the possible negative outcomes of a situation. Reading Eckhart's book, I decided to make a game of differentiating the voices and I started naming them. For example, I have Annie Anxiety and Nellie Negativity. Eckhart suggests the best way to break free from the thoughts in your head is to acknowledge them without fighting them. If you try to ignore or fight the thoughts and voices, they become more powerful. I found making a game of this made it easier to detach from the voices. When I would hear my anxiety and feel it ramp up, I would just say to myself, "That Annie Anxiety is such a worrier." This helped detach my true self from the anxiety and gave me space to feel the anxiety without being overtaken by it. Doing this, I could determine if there was really anything to worry about at all.

Detaching isn't about not feeling; it is about creating some space for you break out of the reaction phase so you can determine whether you need to take any action or whether your thoughts are just trying to take over. Underneath the voices that fight to be heard and are full of anger, anxiety, nervousness, or other unsettling feelings, you will find, eventually, the calm and sure voice. It doesn't need to yell and it often speaks only once. This is the voice of your true self. This is the voice to which you want to practice listening. The only way to begin accessing this voice is by taking the time to let the other voices spin themselves out so you can hear the calm voice. This comes from learning to be quiet within yourself.

As you learn to listen to and detach from the voices, you can start to become truly free. Here is an example. Suppose you are at a wedding reception. Someone asks you to stand up and say something about the bride and groom. On hearing this request, the voices start ramping up! "What if I make a mistake? What if they don't like the way I look? What if I say something they don't like? What if my voice cracks? I don't know what to say and I'm going to look like a fool! This always happens to me!" And the voices go on and on! These are the voices of your past fears: they enjoy their power over you and relish being in control of you. These fears are all from the past, from the times when you were ridiculed or when you were told (or perceived that you were told) you were stupid, not good enough, or ugly.

If you let these voices land, they will take control of you and other voices will join them. The thoughts these voices express can take control of you, freeze you, and keep you small. I look at detaching as not giving the voices a place to land. Not believing them. Keep in mind that whatever you resist will persist. If you try to fight the thoughts, they persist. Saying things like "No, no I'm good. I'm not this. I'm not that." or "I shouldn't be having this voice anymore! I thought I had already dealt with it! Why is it back!?" only leads to the thoughts you're fighting becoming more deeply entrenched. Instead, find a way that works for you to acknowledge the voices, and the thoughts they express, and to let them go through.

When these voices come up, don't believe them and don't give them a place to land. I found acknowledging a voice by its name works for me: "I hear you Annie Anxiety and I know you are worried, but it will be just fine." Another approach—one I heard an instructor at a seminar suggest when talking about detaching from these false voices—is to treat a voice as you would a small child. If you ignore a child, it will get louder and even harder to manage. You can say something like, "I hear you. I know you are upset. I hear you and I feel you, but we need to do this right now." Similarly, you can talk to and reassure one of these voices while still being firm that you are going in a direction other than the one the voice wants you to go. So, for instance, you acknowledge the voice of anxiety and tell that voice you aren't going to go down the path it wants you to go. The way to break free of these voices is by acknowledging, hearing, and feeling instead of ignoring and fighting.

I add the feeling component to the concepts in Eckhart Tolle's *A New Earth.* If you focus only on the voices and thoughts in your head without connecting them to the felt sense of your body, then you may find yourself continuing to fight the same battle over and over again. Remember, some of the triggers causing these reactions may be stored in your body's tissue memory. You need to use feeling to find places holding tissue memory and then release them to free yourself from the battle. Tolle's book is an excellent resource for help in detaching from the ego and in looking at things in a different way. I recommend you read his book and also seek out other books that discuss thoughts, ways they can control us, and ways we can change them.

If you find you can't detach from the message of a particular voice, or you detach again and again but the same issue keeps coming up, you need to check to see if you have places in your body needing release. When you are feeling triggered, make sure you pay attention to what your body is doing. If you can feel a sensation in your body—your stomach clenches or your shoulder tightens—the sensation points you to the place in your body requiring your attention. In a case such as this, you'd want to add the component of bodywork to help free yourself from the triggers and its voice.

Suppose you notice your shoulder tightens every time you start to get anxious. Once you've noticed this, start bringing some attention to your shoulder from time to time to notice how the shoulder feels. Whenever you feel the shoulder start to tighten, bring your full attention to it. See if you can picture what the tissue looks like. Is it a knot, a band, a rope? Does it feel like it is a mass of tangled wire? Visualizing an area can be very helpful in bringing your full awareness to the area.

Sometimes simply bringing your attention to the area is enough to get it to start to release. Continuing our shoulder example, you might need to talk to your shoulder as you would to a young child. Remember the body tightens and braces when it is threatened, whether the threat is real or perceived. So, if your shoulder tightens every time you start to get anxious, your body experiences the anxiety by feeling as if it is under attack. Here are some examples of what you might say to your shoulder. "I hear you. I am safe now; you don't need to tighten any more. It's okay to let go." That may be all your body needs to hear.

You may have hurt your shoulder years ago but it never released completely. So now, every time you feel any threat, the shoulder reacts as if it is being hurt again. Your shoulder may just need to hear the words that it is safe and healed and doesn't need to brace anymore. If the shoulder is still knotted up after you take some time talking to it and breathing into it, this is an indication that the tissue needs actual treatment. You could use some methods of self-treatment to help release the tissue or you might make an appointment to get some treatment done. Know, however, that until the tissue releases, you are likely to continue having the struggle with your anxiety, as your shoulder probably stores some of the tissue memory causing some of your anxiety.

Tightening, clenching, pressure, and pain in your body are all indications of places in which tissue memory is stored. Remember, as you work to release tissue, you may find that physical or emotional sensations, thoughts, or beliefs also come up in the process. In that case, acknowledge and release whatever surfaces. Breaking free is a dynamic and balanced process of freeing yourself from the thoughts, voices, emotions, and physical restrictions that limit you. All of these limiting elements are interconnected and each one needs to be addressed. Keep the words *dynamic* and *interconnected* in mind. No protocol works in each and every situation. I will continue to suggest various approaches throughout this book, but please keep reminding yourself that each situation is unique and the process of freeing yourself always needs to be dynamic.

This would be a good time to for you to repeat the exercises from Chapter 8: *How Do We Listen?* These exercises help you connect to your feelings and discover the ways your body reacts when you are telling the truth and when you are lying. The more you can feel the difference between how your body reacts to your telling the truth and telling a lie, the more you will be able to tell when you are reacting and when you are present.

If you find you can detach easily from your thoughts, you are doing well with that part of this process. If you find you can't detach or you have the same reactions or voices repeatedly, look for physical and emotional aspects that may be keeping you from breaking free. As you progress in this dynamic process, you may feel occasionally like you are losing ground. At such times, it is important to remember and cultivate compassion and grace.

## Chapter 25

# The Gifts of Compassion and Grace

The gifts of compassion and grace are like a gentle hand holding you when you feel like you can't go on. You will need to remember to be gentle with yourself as you progress along your path. When you get frustrated, remember compassion. As you start to use compassion, you will elicit grace in your life. The healing journey is one of cultivating what you want to grow, not of focusing on what you don't like about yourself or about anything else. When you start on your path to uncovering your true self, sometimes you can get caught in the trap of looking only at what you don't like about yourself or of finding only the things you want to change. Uncovering these things is part of our journey, but you also need to remember to start cultivating the things you like about yourself and appreciating the beauty within you and the gifts you bring to this world.

I like to use the term "compassionate honesty" in referring to the nature of the process of self-discovery. You want to start looking at yourself with compassionate honesty. Let go of the concept of brutal honesty, of picking apart everything you do and of focusing constantly on the aspects of yourself that you don't like. When you are triggered or find an aspect that you would like to improve, be gentle with yourself. When you become aware of being triggered or of wanting to change something about yourself, you have become aware of a place in you that holds a fear or a lie, one that you took on in the past and now controls you. Usually, you take on a fear or a lie as a way to protect yourself from being hurt or ridiculed, or to make yourself acceptable and to fit in. So, when you find a place like this in yourself, you've discovered a means by which your fears are controlling you and a place that needs to be healed. Don't use this discovery to beat yourself up even more.

When you start looking at the concept of being true, you will find you have been taught to lie. We are taught it is better to lie than to risk hurting someone's feelings by telling the truth. It starts out with something simple. For instance, when you were little, you might have been told, "I know you don't like Grandma's pies, but eat some and tell her you do anyway. You don't want to hurt her feelings." It seems like an innocent lie, but lies build on each other. Before you know it, you are in a relationship with someone because you don't want to hurt their feelings. In time, you can get so good at lying it can be hard to recognize your truth anymore. Start noticing how much you lie throughout the day. As you catch yourself, just be aware of the lie and the fear that led you to lie. Be compassionate with yourself as you realize how much lying has become a part of your life. Grace will come as you start to speak your truth.

Another aspect of returning to your true self is looking at the intention behind your actions. We were taught to use manipulation to get our desired end result. As with so many of the factors that took us away from our true self in the first place, we learned the manipulation game early. You learn if you act a certain way, you will get a certain response. And, you learn to act in particular ways that get the positive response or the rewards you want.

Some people are really good at using guilt to manipulate others. When you begin looking at the intent behind each of your actions, you may find you really need to be compassionate with yourself. You may discover the motive for your actions often has to do with trying to get something from someone in return—like approval, love, or even a gift—or with trying to make someone will "owe" you in return. You may find you very rarely act purely, without any thought of what you will get in return.

When we were young, we were taught that if we did something "good" we would get a reward. If I cleaned the house, I would get rewarded with praise or money. If I shoveled the drive I might get taken to the movies. Each of us has a list of the ways we were manipulated and the list goes on and on. When you really start to look at the intentions behind your actions, you will see once again how your fears control you. One approach to looking at your intentions is to ask, "Will people like or love me just as I am, or do I have to earn being liked or loved?" Ask yourself this question and see what it brings up for you.

Once we start really looking into our intentions, we find we are not honest. We find we lie a lot, and the intention behind many of our actions is centered on what we can get out of this, what is in it for us. Too often, our intention is to find out—"If I'm nice to this person, what can I get out of it?" As you come to realize most of this comes from your programming, you'll be able to show yourself compassion. We are taught you get love and approval based on what you do and how you act. If you follow the examples, you get love. If you step outside the lines, you can get shunned. Most of life has been learning how we're supposed to behave to get benefits or positive results. When you find yourself doing these things, when you uncover fears, beliefs, and thoughts that keep you from being your true self and cause you to suffer, instead of beating yourself up, look at yourself with compassion. Then the grace of healing and love can enter your life, and you will connect to your authentic self more fully.

I've really liked two of Pema Chödrön's books about grace and compassion, *The Places that Scare You* and *Starting Where You Are*. You will find many other books address this subject too, so be open to finding ones that speak to you. As you start adding the gifts of compassion and grace to your healing process, you will see yourself start to flourish. This is how you tend to your heart and soul: with compassion and grace. Consider the garden analogy again in this light. You want to pull the weeds, but you also want to water and fertilize the plants to help them grow. You want to tend to the gifts inside you and encourage them to grow. Use the same love when you find a weed that you want to remove. Don't curse at it and rip it out saying it shouldn't be there. Of course the weed will try to grow in the garden. It has fertilizer, water, and good soil. Why wouldn't it want to grow there? The same can be said about the fears and lies you have been taught. Your young mind was a perfect place for them to take hold. So, when you find things about yourself that you would like to improve, stop attacking and blaming yourself. Of course you were going to learn to manipulate, judge, and lie. Those are the seeds that were planted. As you become aware of what has been planted, now you have the choice to cultivate what you really want to grow and remove what you don't want.

The next time someone calls and asks you to go to the movie, and you find yourself telling the lie that you already have plans, have compassion. You just lied instead of telling the truth. What if you had told the truth that you just want a quiet night at home? What did you fear? Perhaps you were afraid your truth would hurt the person's feelings. Or, maybe your truth would bring up your belief that you don't deserve a free night. As you look into the lies and truths in a situation like this one, you may be surprised by the number of fears, lies, and thoughts you uncover. You can learn a lot by looking thoroughly at the fears that determine each of your actions.

There are so many different fears that come up with every little interaction we have. You begin to see all these fears as you start looking at yourself compassionately when you catch yourself lying or when you look back on a situation and see your intention wasn't one you would want to cultivate. Once you start to become aware, you then have the power to begin changing; this is when you start to become more empowered. Imagine how different the world would be if each one of us would commit to living with ease and grace instead of in competition and through power, if we rejected the ways we lie and manipulate and, instead, embraced acting out of truth and love. The more compassion you have for yourself, the more compassion you can have for others. When you stop judging yourself so harshly, you will stop judging others. As you love and heal yourself, you can show others how to heal and love too.

Grace will come easily when you are compassionate. Grace is always there; you just need to open up and let it in. If you are guarded or shut down, you are blocking grace from yourself. Grace is like taking a breath of fresh air after you have been stuck in a stuffy, smoky room. It eases your soul and brings gentleness to your heart. Grace comes when you soften, when you take down the walls you have put up between you and others, letting in love.

When you find you are beating up yourself, another way to cultivate compassion and grace up is to put someone else in your shoes. When you find you are looking at yourself with hardness, judgment, or hatred, stop and take a deep breath. Then ask yourself, "If my best friend were to act in this way, or were in this same situation, what would I say to him?" This can be the quickest way to bring compassion to the situation. Notice how harshly you treat yourself; ask yourself if you would treat your best friend the same way. As you become aware of the grace and compassion you would bestow on your friend, see if you can open up to feeling the same way about yourself. You will not be able to be truly compassionate and loving to others until you have compassion and love for yourself. Remember to cultivate compassion and grace in your life; they are truly gifts that will help accelerate your healing journey.

## Chapter 26

*Appreciate, Acknowledge, and Rest*

Along with the gifts of grace and compassion, other gifts can help you cultivate your garden and let your inner beauty shine. Three of these gifts are appreciation, acknowledgement, and rest. To cultivate these gifts, keep in mind you are always at the summit at any given time on your journey. As you progress, you will want to take time to rest so you can restore your energy. Look back and appreciate how far you have come, and, look ahead and acknowledge the path you would still like to take. Know that at any point along your journey, you are already at your summit. Where ever you are, you have already "made it!" Let go of thinking you need to keep looking at where you want to go, of thinking where you are is wrong or limited.

Sometimes it's good to take a seat, appreciate everything you have done, and let yourself rest awhile. This can be a good time to process all you have done and learned so far on your journey. It can be easy to fall into thinking you must always go, go, go, and do, do, do; this mindset is directly opposed to the spiritual practice of being. You have to practice being just like you practice everything else. I love to remind myself we are supposed to be human-beings, not human-doings. Somewhere along the way we lost that philosophy and have taken on instead the belief that you are wasting your time if you aren't doing something.

When you take time for appreciation and acknowledgement, it's an opportunity to notice all the beliefs and habits you have changed by letting go of those that dampened your spirit and embracing now those that enhance your spirit. Try to notice how much or how often you focus on things you consider to be wrong with you or things you are not doing in a way you would like. You want to keep a balance between looking at ways to improve with looking at ways you already have grown; otherwise, you can get caught up in negativity that hinders your growth. You will benefit from having friends who can help you see the ways you have grown, as you may find it easier sometimes to identify your so-called faults than to see your gifts. It's good to be reminded to take a look at all the plants in your garden and see the beauty you have cultivated and grown, instead of just looking for the weeds. Changing your focus in this way can lead to significant growth.

Take time to acknowledge how much you have changed and remember it can take time and conscious effort to change beliefs or thought patterns that have been a part of you for years. Think about this as being like learning to drive in a different country. If you have been driving on the one side of the road your entire life and then you visit a country where they drive on the opposite side of the road, it takes some time and a lot of concentration to change. Your automatic, long-standing habit will make you want to drive on your accustomed the side of the road and it will take conscious effort to override that programming.

It's the same with changing any thought pattern or belief that has become automatic. If we expect ourselves to change without any effort in the healing process, we will just tend to reinforce our negativity about ourselves. We will tend to negative thoughts like, "I failed again." Appreciate the small changes; they are valuable in and of themselves and they will lead you toward bigger and bigger changes. Be open to improving even just 1%. As you do this, you will be amazed at how easy it can be to grow. Acknowledge that the growth process will zigzag and isn't linear. You will go back and forth between an old belief you are trying to change and the new belief you are cultivating.

In some interactions, it will be easy to step into the newer, healthier belief you are cultivating and then you will find yourself reverting to your old beliefs. Does that mean you are not as good as you were the day before or that you've gone backwards? No, it means you have just arrived at another summit along your journey.

Resting is also a very important part of your journey. Resting involves learning to honor the wisdom of taking time to be quiet and to reflect. This is what the Sabbath is all about. The Sabbath is about taking time to rest and nourish your body, spirit, and soul. It's about taking time to fill your spirit by doing things such as: appreciating the flowers, the sunset, or your family; reading sacred scripture or other meaningful books; meditating; and other activities that connect you to the divine more fully. For your overall health and well-being, you need to take time to unplug from the physical world and to enhance your connection with the spiritual world.

Resting is very important, but, in our culture, taking time to rest is not viewed in a positive light at all because resting not productive. We are taught to work hard and unceasingly; this only gets us further entwined in the craziness of the physical world, and we end up missing out on our life. Just compare the European version of a vacation with the United States' version. To Europeans, a typical vacation lasts a month and involves the entire family. In the United States, such a vacation is virtually inconceivable. Widely differing approaches to making rest a part of life also show up in the way people dine in Europe and in the United States. I had personal experience with this difference when I was in Germany. We went out to eat one night and, after a few minutes of waiting for the server, I became agitated because it was taking her so long to get to our table. I kept thinking to myself, "Where is the server!?" I have the mentality of someone from the United States: "We've got to get our food, shovel it in, and get back on the road!" However,

Europeans take their time at meals, time to appreciate conversation with each other, and time to eat and appreciate the meal itself. Many people from the United States have really lost an appreciation for slowing down and for resting.

Another aspect of rest to consider is the difference between rest that enhances your spirit and rest that just numbs the spirit. Sitting on the couch and watching mindless TV does not enhance your spirit; it actually numbs the spirit. When you watch TV, are you watching something that nourishes your soul or one of the crazy reality shows that just bring up more negativity and drama? Can you take time to read a nice book or to sit on a swing and watch the stars?

As you start doing more to nourish your soul in restful ways, also take notice of the thoughts and beliefs that arise. When I first starting taking time to rest and nourish, my mind went into overdrive bringing up all the negative beliefs I had about resting. Growing up on a farm, we were only on the couch when we were really sick. You didn't just lie around; there was work to be done! At first, it was really hard for me to start taking time for rest, but the more I read books on spiritual subjects, the more I noticed some common advice: take time to rest and refresh your spirit. For example, in the New Testament, Jesus demonstrates the need to take time for reconnecting in order to remain connected to your guidance and on your true path. Even though He had thousands of people who wanted his attention, He took time to go out alone in the woods or in the desert to nourish His soul. If He hadn't taken this time to reconnect and rest, He would not have been able to lead the path that He did. If you read various religious and spiritual books, you will find each of those who became a master made it a priority to practice refreshing his or her spirit. If you believe you are always supposed to put others first and yourself last, you will find yourself exhausted and unable to help others. If you don't take time to nourish your soul and to rest your body, you're not going to have the strength or ability to help anyone else or yourself.

Getting a restful sleep is vital to keeping yourself refreshed. Learning how to quiet your mind before you go to bed will help improve the quality of your sleep. When you lie down to go to sleep, if your mind races around the list of things you either did that day or need to do the next day, or you find yourself reliving the activities of the day, your mind will be scattered in all different directions. This will cause tension in your body as you go to sleep. Sleep is supposed to be the time your body rests, heals, and recovers. If your mind is scattered and your body tense when you fall asleep, you're likely to wake up with the same mental and physical state. You will be tense throughout the night and not get the rest you vitally need.

Doing the following exercise can help you get a more restful and restorative sleep.

### Exercise: Restorative Sleep

This exercise helps quiet your body and mind; this in turn can allow your body the time it needs to rest and heal and can help your mind be calm and restful. You can do this exercise in as short a time as a few minutes or you can expand on it to be as detailed as you want or need.

Begin by lying down and taking a few deep breaths, letting your body settle into your bed as you do so. Feel yourself being supported fully by the bed. With each breath, feel your body sinking deeper and deeper into your bed. Let your body get heavy.

When your mind is racing and you are under tension, your body interprets these characteristics as a potential danger, so it is important to let both your mind and your body know each is safe and each can relax and soften.

As you continue to take deep breaths, make some statements to help you relax even more. You can speak out loud or hear the statements in your head. Use any of the following statements or compose ones that work for you.

186

- I am safe now.

- I am fully supported.

- It's okay to let go.

- It's time for my mind and body to rest and heal.

- I give myself permission to let go of all of those things I no longer need to hold.

- I let go of all of the tension and worries from the day.

The statements can be as simple or as complex as you like. Just use the statements that feel right for you at that time. Feel into your body as it softens. Be aware of when your mind starts to go back to your to-do list and just bring yourself back by letting yourself feel your body on the bed again.

You can also give your body and spirit some intentions for while you're sleeping. For example, if you have a stuffy nose, or tension or pain in your body, you can give your body some direction on what you would like it to do to help yourself heal. When you make an intention, use the same guideline as for making a goal: focus on what you want, not on what you do not want. For instance, you might state your intention as, "I want to wake up in the morning and be able to breathe with ease" or "I want to wake in the morning and have my neck move freely." Doing this helps your body and mind know what you would like to do.

If you wake up that next morning and your nose is still stuffy or your neck is still stiff and achy, your body is telling you it did everything it could do but it needs some help from you. In this case, your body is indicating you need to do your part to help with the healing process. You might take more vitamins or take some medicine to help with your nose. You might do some self-treatment or get some treatment to help with your neck.

I have found a statement like the following can be very helpful: "*I give my body permission to do whatever it needs to do* so that when I wake up at 5:30 in the morning I feel refreshed and rested." A statement like this one makes use of the profound influence of your thoughts on your ability to rest and heal, harnessing and channeling your healing ability to achieve the results you want. You can make any kind of intention you like. Making an intention is a way of realizing your power.

As you take this time to make intentions, it's also a good time to visualize a few of your goals.

Play with this exercise for 3 or 4 nights in a row, taking your time with it each time you lie down to sleep. You will see for yourself how much of a difference it can make.

Cultivating the gifts of appreciation, acknowledgement, and rest, along with bringing more grace, compassion, and love into your life, will allow for big jumps in your healing and growth process.

Chapter 27

*Learning to Communicate with Your Body*

Learning to feel into and then communicate with your body is an important and sometimes overlooked part of the healing journey. Earlier in this book, I discussed feeling into and connecting to your body. In this chapter, I illustrate some of these concepts further to help reinforce them. I also bring up some ideas on ways to enhance your communication with your body and how this can help with your healing and growth.

Earlier, I also wrote about how the body communicates through sensations such as pressure, pulling, achiness, pain, and tension. I mentioned the fact that most of us were neither taught how to listen for this communication nor how to make use of it when we did receive it. You may have learned to communicate with your body the way a drill sergeant communicates with a new recruit, you telling the body what to do whether it wanted to it or not. The body's opinions or wants were not taken into account; its protests were futile and sometimes led to punishment. Your relationship with the body was a dictatorship with the communication going only one way: from you to your body. The relationship was sometimes forceful and damaging in nature. If you were taught the "No pain, no gain" philosophy, when your body did express hurt, you may have just kept on going. You were taught to keep pushing through the pain, to turn it off, or to medicate and cover it.

Not having learned how to communicate with the body, you may have pushed to the point of injuring yourself. If you sought help for your pain or injury, you might have been given medicine to try to cover the pain or have been taught some strengthening or stretching exercises. Medication and exercises can be helpful, but often these lead to only temporary relief and you continue to have problems or to reinjure the area. If you continued to have problems, you eventually were told the aches and pains "are just part of the aging process." You were told you would "have to learn to deal with it," which means becoming a lifelong pill taker.

Another option you might have been given is surgery. Sometimes surgery is necessary, but it should always be the last option, as it is invasive and leads to further damage. Often in our healthcare system, surgery is proposed as the first option for responding to pain, dysfunction, or injury. Surgery can lead to a lot of unnecessary damage to your body. Every surgery, no matter how minor (for example, removing tonsils or wisdom teeth) is considered a life-or-death trauma from the body's perspective.

When I hear talk about the "normal aging process," I like to throw out some food for thought. That a majority of people have more pain as they age doesn't mean increased pain with aging is normal or should be accepted as inevitable. Before we were taught how to care for our teeth effectively, it was "normal" for people's teeth to rot and decay by an early age. Once we learned how to help to prevent tooth decay, a new "normal" occurred; people expected to have healthy teeth for a much longer time and decay became abnormal. The same can be true for our bodies.

When we learn and apply better health practices, we can make significant reductions in the amount of pain and decay that occur in the body over time. Learning self-treatment methods can help decrease or eliminate the accumulation of stress and trauma. Self-treatment is much more beneficial than is any approach that simply tries to cover up the symptoms of stress and trauma. After an injury or a trauma, you can begin self-treatment by applying the universal principles to your body in order to regain balance and elasticity. Learning how to work with your body to release it from the buildup of tension is equivalent to learning how to brush and floss your teeth to remove the buildup of tarter and food. The results of this approach to working with your body can be just as dramatic, in terms of preventing decay and maintaining health, as the results of brushing and flossing your teeth. Learning how to communicate with your body can help guide you to knowing what it needs in order to maintain and restore health

When the body sends out the sensations like pain and pressure, it is trying to guide you to areas needing help. If you do not listen, and you keep pushing and forcing, your body starts to protect itself by locking down. As the body locks down, movement becomes restricted. The pain then increases and causes the body to lock down more. Before long, this cycle begins to limit your function.

When you notice limits in your function—along with pain and restricted movement—you may start to get frustrated with your body because you can no longer function the way you would like to do. You want to blame your body for falling apart; it has let you down. On the other hand, the body feels like you have been forcing it to do things that hurt and harm it; when it tries to tell or guide you about forcing it, you don't listen. Pretty soon, it's like your mind and body are at war with each other. You've been pushing your body, forcing and abusing it with your activities and sometimes even with the exercises and treatments you were told were supposed to help it. Your body has been trying to communicate with sensations, but its communications aren't heeded in a way that alleviates the problems, so it locks up more and more to protect itself.

This war between mind and body becomes cyclic. You want to continue to function, so you keep forcing because you don't know what else to do, even though it's causing harm. From your body's point of view, you are abusing it and not listening to it, so it locks down to protect itself from you, the abuser. If you haven't been taught an effective way to communicate with your body and you use a dictatorial approach with it, then, from the body's point of view, you have abused and neglected it by not helping to alleviate the problems that are causing tissue damage.

So how do you start restoring a healthy communication between your mind and body? Look at it as starting a negotiation process between two warring countries. Your mind and body have been at war with each other, sometimes for a very long time. The warring stems from the mind and the body misunderstanding each other's communications. Over time, the results of these misunderstood communications have escalated the war.

Your mind and body speak different languages. This is the root of their misunderstanding each other's communications about injury and trauma. Each has been communicating in its native tongue, expecting the other to understand what it is saying. Unaware of this difference in languages, when the mind and body fail to communicate, each believes the other *can* understand but is *choosing* not to listen. So, each decides to talk louder, and, before long, each side is shouting at the other, each believing the other is being deliberately contrary. To change this destructive cycle, each side needs to start to learn the other's language; this will enable true communication. Mind and body also need to build trust in one another. As with countries that have been at war for a long time, building trust will take patience and effort from both sides, an openness on each side to hear the other side's needs, and a willingness to forgive and understand.

To learn how your body communicates, you have to learn how to listen to the body's language. I gave some exercises on how to start connecting with and listening to your body in Chapter 8: *How Do We Listen?* I will reinforce here some of the key concepts concerning listening to your body. As you start to communicate with your body, you will be able to tell when you are helping it heal and when you may be causing more tightness or damage. When you attempt to help release your body, you want to work with it, not force it. Helping your body release involves connecting with it and allowing it to open up. Listening to your body as you self-treat will allow you to help free it; forcing your body as you self-treat can cause it to lock down even more.

As you help your body release, breaking free of its restrictions, it will be able to move more easily. In this way, both mind and body get what they want. This is how you start establishing trust between mind and body, which improves communication and leads to even better results. This is the cycle you want to establish and maintain, the cycle that leads to ease of movement, not the one that causes you to lock up more and more. Applying the universal principles to your self-treatment program, and being treated by therapists who follow those principles (for example, therapists who have been taught JFB-MFR), is a way to establish and develop trust between your mind and your body, while at the same time freeing your body from the restrictions that are locking it down.

As you go about your daily activities, start to become aware of when your body is communicating with you. Notice when you start to feel sensations and then acknowledge those sensations. This is the first line of communication: acknowledging the sensations as they occur. Sometimes all the body needs is your acknowledgement. For example, suppose you are sitting at your desk and your body's alarm system indicates something is going on with your hip. The condition in your hip is just starting and doesn't seem dire, so your body sends out a low level alarm: the sensation of pressure. Now it's your turn. If you acknowledge the pressure and address it at this level, the alarm may not need to get any louder. If you ignore the pressure, then the alarm will get louder and spread.

It's your job to go check out what is going on when an alarm goes off. To do this, bring your full attention into the area where the alarm is sounding. Breathe into your hip and feel what is happening there. See if there is tension or tightness in the hip. Check the environment to see how it might be influencing the hip. You might find you are sitting on something uneven and all you need to do is adjust your seat.

If you feel tension in your muscles, acknowledge the tightness and give your body permission to soften. Sometimes all your body needs is the permission to soften. Your body may have been bracing and tense from an old injury or trauma, and it has just needed the "all clear" signal. So, sometimes all the body needs is for you to just feel where you're bracing or tight and then to give the body permission to soften and let go. If it remains tense after you do this, you might need to adjust your seat or get up and relieve the pressure. You don't necessarily have to take a long break. Sometimes all your body needs to get a little relief is just two or three minutes of moving in the opposite direction. If you learn to start taking little breaks when your body first starts to get sore or tight, you can really help prevent the sore or tight area from getting so painful that it locks down. Another way you could try to help release the pressure is by putting a ball or treatment tool on the tight spot.

If your situation does not allow you to give your body a break or to treat it at the moment, then be honest with your body; again, make use of communication. Let your body know you hear it and you are sorry you can't alleviate the tension at this moment. Then set a time when you will be able to take a break or treat it. For example, you might say, "I will be able to get out of this chair in an hour and then I will walk around and help loosen you up." You might say, "When I get home at 4:00 today, I will be able to do some self-treatment to help you release." Self-treatment is crucial to helping yourself heal and this is why it is important to work with a therapist who can show you how to self-treat.

When you follow through by doing what you tell your body you are going to do, you start to build a trusting relationship with your body. As you build trust with your body, your body will start talking to you in a quieter voice. It will send tension instead of always jumping to the sensation of pain or needing to lock down. This is one of the ways to start developing a healthy communication with your body:

acknowledging the sensations as they come up; feeling into the tissue; and giving the tissue permission to soften. If you take this approach in a particular instance and the body is able soften, then all it needed was your acknowledgement. If it can't soften, take some action or plan a time when you can do something to help alleviate the pressure and tightness.

Now that I have talked about listening to the body when it sends signals, I will discuss communicating with the body as a way to help open up the spots that call for your attention. Remember, it is about opening up or freeing up your body in a way that is not forceful. You want to work with your body. To open up in this way, use the moving awareness exercise I gave in Chapter 8. Refer to that chapter for details on this exercise. In short, start moving your body three-dimensionally; don't use a pattern or routine, just move freely and explore all motions. As you move, feel where your tissue moves freely and where it is tight or locked down. Anywhere you feel knots or restrictions is a place that needs to be treated using the universal principles of engaging, holding, and allowing.

As you start to open up the places that are locked down, you'll be preventing pain and achiness. You'll also be telling the body you're taking care of it, that keeping yourself open and mobile is a priority. You'll be showing the body you want it to feel good, and this starts to build a relationship of trust. Using these movement exercises to find where you need to treat is another way to become empowered in your healing process. Instead of going to someone to have them tell you where you need to treat, you will find those places for yourself.

Another way to communicate with your body is through visualization. Make it a part of your practice to visualize some of your goals. Visualize some functional goals you would like to attain, such as walking with ease, reaching overhead easily, or gardening. See yourself moving with fluidity and ease, smiling and enjoying yourself, so you can let your body know you want to do these things but you also want it to feel good at the same time. Previously, you may have had goals but also have had the mindset that you would attain those goals at any cost, even if attaining the goals hurt your body.

You can also visualize personal growth goals, such as staying centered when you speak in front of a group or being at ease when you are taking a test. You can also use visualization to help your body prepare for potentially stressful situations. The next time you have a doctor's a dentist's appointment, let your body know ahead of time what is going to be done at the appointment. It is especially important to give the body an idea ahead of time if the appointment will involve any procedures. If you're going to the dentist, visualize sitting in the chair. As you visual this, let your body know your teeth are going to be cleaned or cavities may need to be filled, especially if you're going to be getting an injection, having blood drawn, or having surgery. Let the body know what's going on and why; this helps keep it from thinking it's going to get cut, poked, and prodded for no apparent reason other than to be tortured or hurt. You need to remember that, in the past, your body has seen such things as being hurt for no apparent reason. These hurts from the past, which seemed to the body to have been attacks, are part of the reason the body is braced all the time; it doesn't know what will happen next. Using visualization to help prepare the body will also help it trust you more and more.

Using visualization can also help the body guide you to places that need treatment in the process of attaining your various goals. For instance, you can visualize a goal like walking with ease and then ask your body, "Where do I need to treat in order to progress towards this goal?" Quiet down and open yourself up for guidance. Sometimes your body communicates with you using a twitch, an ache, or a throb. Sometimes you'll get a picture of putting the small therapy ball somewhere on your hip or you'll just get a flash of a self-treatment picture that you've been shown before. These are just some of the ways your body may communicate to help guide you to where you need to treat. All of these are ways you can start to develop a relationship with your body as a partner instead of as a dictator.

Remember to take time to self-treat and to do things that feel good to your body. Ask for your body's input on all activities. Ask your body what foods it wants and listen when it says it has had enough. If you want to know whether an activity might either help or harm your body, just ask. The body will not let itself be injured without resisting, so if you're doing some type of self-treatment or stretch that you were taught and your body actively resists it, your body is telling you that exercise or stretch is too much for it right now. If your body can soften into what you are doing, then you are helping it; if it can't, back off some and see if that helps. If it still is resisting, stop the exercise or stretch for now. Just because you can take the pain doesn't mean that it's good or healthy for you, or, if you're being treated, that the therapist isn't causing your body to tighten down even more. Whether you're treating yourself or being treated by someone, listen to your body.

If you feel pain during treatment or self-treatment, breathe in and feel the place that is being treated. If you can feel the tissue softening, opening, and giving, the body is telling you the treatment is helping even though it is painful. The treatment might be breaking up scar tissue or adhesions, or it might be bringing up pain from tissue memory; these kinds of pain need to be released for you to heal. If a muscle contracts where you are treating or being treated, that is the indication too much force is being applied and the amount of pressure needs to be backed off. To understand these concepts thoroughly, I would highly recommend working with a therapist who understands them. Such a therapist can help you to feel your body's various responses to treatment and the differences between those responses.

When your body hurts, when you feel pain, you may brace; but, even if you're bracing, you should still be able to feel the tissue softening and giving. There's a difference between bracing and a muscle actively contracting. If you're not sure what you're feeling during treatment, actively contract the muscle in the area being treated, keep contracting it for three or four seconds, and then let it go. When you stop contracting the muscle, if it lets go completely it's telling you the pressure is okay. If the muscle can't let go when you stop contracting it, and it stays contracted against what's going on, it's telling you there's too much force. If you're still not sure after doing this, ease the pressure slightly and feel your body's response. It's better to use a little less force than to provoke the body's defenses by being overly forceful. The best way to get a true feeling for this is under the guidance of a therapist trained in this philosophy, specifically someone trained in JFB-MFR.

Learning how to listen to your body is a *very* important part of your healing process. Learning how to communicate to your body using words, movement, and visualization is a vital aspect of healing and of uncovering your truths. At every step, the most important component is taking time. Take time to listen, time to self-treat, time for breaks when your body needs them. You need to change the mentality that once you start a task, you have to finish it no matter what happens along the way.

It's amazing how much can help to take five minute breaks here and there, to take your body out of a stressful situation or position. If you are bent forward working on a computer all day, it can be very beneficial to take time to relieve the pressure of that posture by stretching backwards. In this situation, it's even more helpful to take time to lie down and stretch out. If you're out raking leaves, take five minute breaks now and then; stretch yourself out, even lying down and opening up your chest and shoulders. If you take those five or ten minute breaks throughout the day, you will feel much better at the end of the day. Those breaks make a big difference and make the next parts of the day easier. If you take that five or ten minute break, instead of your body starting to hurt more and more throughout the day, you can finish your day feeling good instead of feeling miserable.

As you progress along your healing journey, sooner or later you will push your body too far. When this happens, your body may react due to the pain and also possibly to fear, which may cause it to lock down completely. You may think you've gone back to square one, but you haven't done that. This is an opportunity that will allow more healing to occur. The only way to know your boundaries is to test them. When you push it too far and it hurts, you might be bringing up an opportunity to release feelings of frustration, sadness, or anger stemming from the physical pain and limited function of your body. Your body may express frustration built up from all the times it was pushed too hard; you may feel frustration at not being able to do the activities you have wanted to do. Emotions are involved in every experience and expressing them will be a part of the healing process.

When you're feeling the results of pushing too hard, remind yourself you are always doing the best you know how to do. In the past you often forced yourself and were forced because that is what you thought was the "right" way. You did all the stretches and exercises you had been taught to try to keep healthy or to heal yourself; you just didn't know the aspect of taking your time and not forcing. Often, those stretches, exercises, and treatments lead to only temporary results or even caused more problems. Now that you know another way, you can start to help truly free up your body. But, in the learning and healing process, you will often fall back into old habits and force too much, causing a flare up. Again, this is a learning process, and it will take time. Be gentle with yourself. Listening and feeling into your body, and learning how to communicate with it, are important steps. Taking these steps will then allow you to make choices and take action that will propel you along your healing journey.

# Chapter 28

## Choices and Actions

Some people believe you have to know the outcome of a decision before you make a choice. This belief keeps people spinning in the cycle of thinking, "I just don't know for sure what I am supposed to do" or "What if I make a mistake?" If you think that everything has to be clear and that you need to know exactly the outcome will be before you act, you will never act. If you wait for perfection before you act, you will never act. If you wait until the path is perfectly clear and there are no obstacles, you will never move. This is another way that your ego takes hold and keeps you from healing.

The fear of making mistakes, of doing things wrong, of taking the wrong path, can paralyze the growth process. What if you could open up to the belief that there is no wrong choice or path? Operating from this belief, you might take a path that later you decide you wouldn't take again, but taking that path wasn't a mistake because you grew while you were on it. You can never miss your one opportunity. If you are meant to go down a particular path, it will come to you again if you miss it. You can't miss your opportunity. This is the cyclical nature of life. No matter what path you take, no matter what step you take, it will lead you towards growth. Life is not static; life is not stable. Life is full of motion, action, cycles. So, if you don't know where to go, it's okay. Just take a step, test the waters, and see what happens. If you have to backtrack later because you want to go down a different path, that's okay and you've still learned something. No path is ever a mistake.

Who would you be if you weren't afraid of making a mistake? Consider that question in light of professional athletics. In baseball, batting over 35% is exceptionally good. In basketball, shooting over 40% is fabulous, which means shooters miss at least 60% of the time. Yet they are considered elite athletes and make millions of dollars, in spite of all the mistakes they make! What if meteorologists were afraid of making a mistake? How often are their weather predictions actually right? They have all the best in radar and satellite technology, and they can still predict a nice sunny day that turns out to be a blizzard! It is very difficult to predict the weather because there are so many variables that can't be controlled.

Trying to predict what may happen in our lives is similar to trying to predict the weather. There are so many variables to every decision we make. Trying to predict the end result of every decision is impossible. Setting your goals puts out what you would like to have happen, but you really can't control all the variables. You could have all kinds of readings done, you could check out your past lives, you can buy all kinds of crystals and do all kinds of ceremonies, but you still can't control or predict the outcome of your actions because you don't know what is meant to happen in your life. The unknown factor of what is meant to happen in your life is necessary for true growth to occur. Knowing this will lead you to believing in yourself no matter what all the expert predictions may say. This is the development of faith and trust in yourself.

Thomas Edison gives a great example on how to change your perspective on mistakes or failures. Edison was asked if he ever got frustrated because he made so many mistakes while trying to find what would work to harness electricity. He said that when he used something that didn't work, he didn't think of it as a mistake but as being one step closer to finding out what would work. What if you looked at life that way? Instead of getting upset because you made a mistake (that is, you didn't get the outcome you wanted), what if you looked at the experience as learning something and thus being one step closer to finding out what would work. What if you had the philosophy that there are not mistakes only missed opportunities?

Just take a minute to look back on some of the times when you didn't act because you were afraid of what might happen. What if you had taken the risk and called that person and told them what you felt about them? What if you had crossed the dance floor and asked that person you had a crush on to dance? If they didn't feel the same or didn't want to dance, could you look at it as an opportunity you are proud to have taken instead of thinking of it as a mistake? At least you were living.

You will never grow if you don't take chances. Life is what happens while you are analyzing the possibilities and researching the possible outcomes. You have to get in and test the waters. Sometimes you can just dip your toe in, but other times you just have to dive in. Sometimes the water will be cold, and you'll want to get right out. Other times you'll find the water feels amazing, and you splash around and have a fabulous time. Either way, you're living!

If you have been hurt, you may feel it is safer to keep your heart walled off than to open yourself up to be hurt again. The truth is the walls you built have trapped your heart in the hurt. The only way to heal and to let love in is to open up. You may think the only options are to either wall off your heart or to be totally open and vulnerable, but there are many options. One option I like to use is the visualization of shutters or blinds around the heart. These are easy to open and you can control how much they are open or closed. You can open the blinds just a little bit to see how it feels, and you have the ability to close them again easily. You can open them as long as you want to let in sunlight, and, if it feels like you want to just close them for a little while, you can do that too.

As with every part of your healing journey, remember you don't have to do it all at once. You can test the waters. You have the ability to open and close yourself up as much as you want and it doesn't have to be hard. Actually, doing this can be easy. It gives you the opportunity to become aware of all the fears and beliefs keeping you from opening yourself up. You can control how much you let come up at any given time and process it as you go. Healing is a balance of stillness and action. It is good to take time to process, set your intentions, and listen for guidance. Then, when it's time to move, move forward. If you aren't sure what to do, try a step and see what happens. You can stay still and wait, not grow, not change, not move, or you can take a step forward. The only way to start to heal and to grow is to start moving and to start living more fully.

You also choose what you perceive in any situation. Sometimes a person gets stuck in her healing process because she can't let go of the right and wrong of a situation involving another person. She wants the other person involved to see the situation the same way she does, to have the same perception she does. Each person's perspective is different because it is based on her previous experiences and her beliefs.

Ten people can be involved with the exact same situation and come back with ten different perceptions of what happened. For example, suppose this group of ten people walks down a road and they meet someone coming from the other direction. Two people look at that other person and feel fear based on the other person's clothing: he's wearing a long trench coat. Another person looks at the stranger and is reminded of an uncle he likes, so he feels friendly toward the stranger. Another person in the group happens to look at the stranger as the stranger is looking down at his feet; this person in the group instantly thinks the stranger is stuck up.

This example points out that each person has his own perception based on his experiences, beliefs, and thoughts. Trying to make someone else see something from your point of view is like trying to make someone love the same kind of ice cream you do. The other person might or might not like it, but you can't make him change his perspective if it's not his truth.

When you are aware of how your perspectives can cause you to judge a situation and in turn possibly keep you from healing, you have some choice about how to proceed. With this awareness, you now have more power in your ability to heal, instead of being ruled by your perspectives. Being willing to open yourself up to seeing different perspectives can be a very powerful tool in healing. For instance, in conflict with someone else, can you see the situation from the other person's point of view? Can you adopt her perspective? Can you see how you are judging her actions, thoughts, or beliefs about various aspects of the situation and open to the possibility that you have done, thought, or believed the same thing, though perhaps in a different way? Taking this approach to the situation doesn't mean you are playing the martyr, saying the conflict is entirely your fault and you are to blame. Usually, if you can see yourself from the other person's perspective, you can find some common ground from which to reach some healing on your part. The other person is responsible for her choice to heal or not. So, let go of the need for agreement; the goal is to reach a point where you can heal yourself. As long as you hold onto the belief that a situation was wrong or shouldn't have happened, you can never heal fully.

You help yourself heal when you let go of the need to have your perception be the right one. This is a powerful tool that can help you forgive not only others, but also yourself. When you think about a past situation for which you know you are still punishing yourself, try switching your perspective. Put a loved one in the same situation and see if you would judge him in the same way. Usually, we are much harder on ourselves than we are on others. And, until you can learn to forgive yourself, it will be hard to forgive others.

So, when you find yourself in a situation in which you can't get past blame or can't get to forgiveness or healing, switch the situation around and be open to see a different perspective. In making every decision you've made at every stage of your life, you've done the best you knew how to do with the information you had at the time. Do your previous choices mean you wouldn't make different choices now or in the future? No, making different choices is the result of learning and growing. And, choosing something different now from what you chose in the past doesn't make your past choice something you shouldn't have done. Take this perspective on past and current choices with yourself and with others. When you can truly see yourself in another person, growth and healing can occur.

Changing your perspective, making choices, taking action, healing— these words all refer to action. I have said this previously, but I repeat it here because it is essential: healing is an active, participatory process. As with active, participatory sports, healing doesn't happen sitting on the sidelines. It won't happen if you are worried about staying clean (not making a mistake), afraid of contact with others (life is a full-contact sport), or if you are worried about being hurt (injuries will happen). You will be injured; you will injure others. Sometimes you will bump deliberately into others; sometimes they will bump deliberately into you; and sometimes you run into each other and you don't even mean to do so!

To heal, you need to get be willing to uncover what is messy, feeling the things you didn't or don't want to feel, facing the situations you didn't or don't want to face. When you take this kind of action, the real growth occurs. This is getting off the bleachers (the place from which you can judge those out on the playing field) and getting into the action (where you open yourself up to be judged by others). And, just like in sports, you can go from being the hero loved by all to the scapegoat booed off the court. Engaging this way and having these kinds of experiences is necessary so that you can learn to play just for yourself.

When you act and make choices, you get out of the books and get into living. The books, the lectures, the various meditations can all help you with the mental understanding; truth comes from the living. You're never going to read yourself into healing. The reading will help give you some guidance and some possible ideas, but the true growth and healing comes from the living. No one can heal you. You have to make the active choice to heal; *you* have to make that choice. You have to ask yourself, "Am I going to hang on to this? Am I going to stay here at this point? Am I going to continue to carry this, or, am I going to move forward?" The choice is all yours, and you are the only one who is responsible for your own healing.

I like the following two stories about taking action.

There was a woman, Ann, who wanted to win the lottery. Every night she would pray to God asking for help in winning the lottery because she knew that if she could only win the lottery, all her troubles would vanish. She even bargained with God that if she won the lottery she would donate a lot of the money to good causes. This went on for over 10 years and she prayed every night. One night as she was praying, again asking God to help her, and questioning why he hadn't helped her yet, she heard God's voice say, "Ann, if you want to win the lottery, then you need to buy a lottery ticket."

The second story goes like this:

A river was flooding its banks, and the residents of a town were evacuating. A sheriff's truck came to Tom's house and offered him a ride to dry ground. Tom declined the ride saying, "I have faith and I know that God will save me." The river continued to rise, and soon Tom had to go to the second level of his home. A boat came by and the people offered to take Tom to safety. Again he declined saying, "I have faith and I know that God will save me."

The waters continued to rise, and now Tom was forced to the roof of his house. A helicopter came to his house and they offered to take him to safety. Again Tom declined saying, "I have faith and I know that God will save me." The waters continued to rise, and Tom was swept away and died. When he arrived in heaven, he asked God angrily, "I had faith in you God, why didn't you save me?!" God replied, "I sent a truck, a boat, and a helicopter. What else did you want?"

We have to do our part in the healing process. Set your goals, ask for help, and then it's up to you to get in and get dirty doing your work. It is truly up to you. When you really step into that truth, the truth that you are responsible and you have the power to help yourself heal, you can become truly empowered and free. It's not up to anyone else! You don't have to wait until you get someone else's forgiveness before you can heal; it's about forgiving yourself. It doesn't matter what has been done to you; it's what you choose to do with it. You have the absolute power and control over your healing and growth. How great is that?!

# Chapter 29

## *Surrendering and Gratitude*

When I used to think about the words "surrender," "to surrender," or "surrendering," I thought they referred to giving up or failing; surrender seemed like a sign of weakness. Part of the healing process is coming to terms with the true meaning of surrender. You may have been taught, like I was, that to give up, surrender, or quit was one of the biggest failures possible. I was taught you're supposed to power your way through; this idea is especially common in our Western culture. You're taught you've got to make things happen, you've got to be forceful, you need to bend the world into what you want it to be. True surrendering is when you come to the realization that there is a power greater than you that connects the entire universe, and that, if you open yourself up to this force by surrendering, you can have more strength and become more empowered than you ever thought possible. Surrender is accepting the fact that you'll always get what you need, not always what you want, and giving up the thought that you always know what is best. It's coming to the understanding that you'll always be provided with what you are meant to receive.

Surrendering also includes accepting the fact that you are already perfect the way you are, that at your core, your soul, you are a brilliant reflection of the divine, or God. It's about accepting that your part of growth includes clearing off the excess to reveal your brilliance. Surrendering is also about learning to trust the process, to trust in the divine, and to trust in yourself.

When I say trust the divine, I don't mean trusting in a specific religion, although it may mean that to some people. Not all religions have to do with connecting to your own divine nature. Some religions focus more on following rules that man has created and on telling people that they are not divine. In every religion, and in every religious book, there are some amazing truths that are from the divine—universal truths—and then there are rules and limits that have been put on by man. The forms of religion and spirituality that lead you to connect to, and be guided by, the divine—and to focus on expanding your spirit—are ones that will lead to healing and growth. The forms of religion and spirituality that focus on fear will actually decrease your connection to the divine and will hinder your healing and growth.

Surrendering is also about letting go of your resistance so you can feel your fears to the core. It's learning how to face your fears continually, until they no longer have power over you. Instead of fighting what you fear, instead of working so hard to try to make sure that what you fear doesn't happen, you need to face and feel your fears fully. You need to surrender to your fears fully. The fastest way to the core is to ask yourself, "What is the worst that could happen if this came true?" When you feel it through and know that even if this worst thing happened, it would be okay—know that your current path is the right path for you, no matter what the outcome—then you are truly free.

The children's book *The Monster in My Closet*, by Eric Klug, is a brilliant example of this process. The child is scared to look in the closet because he is sure there is a monster in there. In the end, when he opens the closet, he finds the only thing he was afraid of was himself. Our fears hold us back, and as you face your fears, you will find out that the only thing giving your fears power is you. I also like a quote on this same topic: "When you stop being afraid of dying, you stop being afraid of living." When you come to terms with the fact that everyone and everything will die, then you stop living in fear of death. At that point, you truly are free to live fully in the present moment.

Surrender is about letting yourself feel the things you are trying not to feel. We work so hard trying not to feel. "I'm going to fight to my last breath trying to make myself happy so I don't have to feel my sadness or anger. I'm going to make myself be peaceful—even though my world might be falling apart—because if I work harder, if I force it to happen, then I will find happiness and peace." The peace and the happiness will come after you surrender to the fact that you are not happy (or let yourself feel whatever emotion or sensation you are trying not to feel). When you stop trying to be somewhere you aren't, or to feel some way that you don't feel, when you surrender and just feel what is there, then you can move through. After you let all the emotions and sensations flow through you, after you feel them to the core and release them, once the fight is over, then you can open yourself up to the peace that comes in the quiet. The turbulence comes from the fighting.

Swimming is a good analogy for this. If you struggle when you are swimming, you'll sink. If you let go and trust that you will be supported, you will float. To me, this is surrendering. Letting go of the needless fight and letting myself be supported. Your task is recognizing when you need to work and when you are just in a needless struggle. If you aren't sure which to do, just try one of the two, working or surrendering. If the one you choose doesn't seem to be working, try the other. This is the action part.

I will use another swimming analogy to help with this idea. If you find yourself in a riptide, your first instinct will probably be to fight against it. As you struggle, you will reach a moment when you realize that the work you are doing is actually making things worse. It's time to surrender. Surrender and rest while the riptide takes you along; then, the moment you feel it lessening, swim. So when you find yourself fighting, fighting, fighting and everything seems to be fighting back against you, it's time to stop and see if you need to surrender. As you take this approach more and more, it will become easier to keep the balance between doing your part and surrendering. Connecting to your true self, healing, and growing are all about balancing between doing your part and surrendering to the bigger plan.

The act of surrendering can go hand with hand with the philosophy of changing your perspective. When you stop fighting, it will be easier to open yourself up to seeing options and ideas you can't see when you are in the midst of a fight. This can be hard to do when you are in the middle of the situation, and, in such times, it is a good idea to have someone you trust help you see options you may not be able to see. To grow, you need to have people in your life who will be honest with you. If all your friends will always agree with what you do or say, then you will have a hard time seeing the places you need to grow. You need people whom you can ask, "Is there anything I am not seeing?" You need people to whom you can say, "Help me see what I can't see right now; help give me a different perspective." The feedback of true friends is essential and a vital part of your growth process.

Gratitude is a gift that can lead to growth and healing. Can you be grateful for your gifts and also for your struggles? Caroline Myss says that it's easy to have gratitude at a banquet table when your belly is full and all the people around you are ones you love and everyone in your family is healthy and happy. The real power of gratitude comes if you can be grateful when you are hungry, tired, and feel abandoned. Those who have reached that level of mastery can see that every phase of life is how it is supposed to be and can practice gratitude in every situation. It doesn't mean that they are enjoying the hunger as much as they enjoy the feast; it's that they have let go of the judgment that the feast is right and the famine is wrong.

To truly heal and grow, you need all aspects to come into your life. Can you be thankful to both sides, as both lead to growth? The times of abundance and scarcity both lead to appreciation of what you have in your life. You need to have both love and loss to clear your fears around love and to be able to practice unconditional love.

Ask yourself if you can be grateful for each of the following.

- People will help you see your gifts and will show you love. Other people will point out your limitations and faults, and will withhold their love. Both are needed so you can understand love is always there and isn't based on who you are or what you do. The people who behave in each of these ways will help you to give and receive the gift of true unconditional love.

- People will give you support and will help you find your strength when you are weak. Other people will test your strength and will pull away when you need them. Both will help you trust fully that you will always be supported and helped; you just need to let go of the idea that you know how that should look.

- People will lift you up when you doubt yourself. Other people will criticize you when you are unsure. Both will help you clear away all your doubts so you can truly learn to trust in yourself.

- There will be times in your life when you are healthy and times when you are sick. There will be times when you can move with grace and ease and times when your body hurts. Both of these will help you to appreciate the gift of your body. They will also help you have compassion for those who are sick or suffer physical ailments.

- You will have many losses in your life. These losses can teach you to believe that the only time you truly lose someone is when you shut them out of your life, the only time you will be without love is when you shut love out, and the only time you feel lacking at all is when you are trapped in the fear of scarcity.

- There will be times when you were forced, abused, and hurt. This will give you the ability to bring the gifts of surrender and forgiveness into your life. This can also help you believe that when hurt and trauma happen to you, you don't have to let them define you.

When you can see the gift in something that you once thought was a tragedy or was "wrong," then you have healed that aspect of your life. When you come to a point in your growth that you can recognize what once seemed to be a tragedy or a wrong as a gift and be grateful for it, then you have freedom.

So, if you find yourself wanting to blame others, or to hold onto things that shouldn't have happened in your life, that is okay. You will do it as long as you need to do it in order to heal what you need to heal. If you want to grow, make a list of anything in your life that you see as "wrong" or that you know you are having a hard time releasing. Then, see if you can open yourself to the possibility of seeing any gifts that occurred because of these things. It may be hard to see the gifts and there may be a part of you that doesn't want to admit that anything good could come from them. Just acknowledge and be kind to yourself in your current state. Don't force anything, but just open the door for your spirit to come and help you with gratitude and healing. You will help free yourself as you are able to open yourself and start to heal the parts of your experience that you feel were wrong or for which you want to blame others. Start practicing gratitude in areas that are easy and then expand from there. When you reach a state in which you can bring gratitude in every aspect of your life, then you are becoming a true master.

Chapter 30

*Reaction of Others*

Our healing and our growth toward becoming our real self can be very significantly limited by falling into the trap of allowing ourselves to be controlled by what other people will think about us, how they will react to us, or how they will judge us. Earlier in this book, I discussed in detail some of the reasons we are concerned about the opinions of others. Most of us have been taught since we were little to change what we feel, think, say, and do in order to keep those around us happy or comfortable. Some of the biggest fears we were taught center on what could happen if we did something considered wrong: we could be kicked out of the family, judged to be unlovable, or abandoned by those we love. We were taught that the people who we thought loved us would turn against us and ridicule us if we made a mistake. In the extreme, if we did something "bad" enough, we could even be put in prison, exiled, or killed.

Fears of this sort can lead to significant fear of being your true self—the consequences could be emotionally and physically devastating, even fatal. How many times as a kid did you get ridiculed for making mistakes or trying something new? This emotional censure continues into our adulthood. Just look at the show *America's Funniest Videos.* As a society, we think it's funny when people hurt themselves. Our entertainment comes from laughing at people who make mistakes and even who have been hurt. Because of this, most people are more afraid of being embarrassed than of dying.

Is it really funny to see someone get hurt? We teach with this attitude that if you trip and fall in front of others, it's better to jump right back up and say, "I'm okay. I'm fine." even if you are really hurt. The lesson is that when you get hurt, it's better to pretend you aren't hurt and to make fun of yourself. Operating from this belief, we compound our physical pain with an emotional one that we cause ourselves. Denying we are hurt reinforces the mentality that "I deserved to be hurt." All of this is based on our reaction to what others think. We would rather suffer our pain without a sign than risk being ridiculed or judged.

When you are on your journey of revealing your true self and you start acting in ways that are true to you instead of doing what you have been told you should do, people will start to notice the changes. Some people won't like how you've changed. If you hear someone say, "I don't know who you are anymore." then you know that you have started to change. Your changing can be very scary for the people around you. You may not fit anymore into the little box where they had put you. You are starting to become the real you, which may go against the perception they had of you.

A great book by Don Miguel Ruiz, called *The Mastery of Love,* addresses the topic of true love and describes the nature of real relationships. It's a book I recommend to everyone. In the book, Ruiz states that we are only responsible for our part of any relationship, for our 50%. All we can do is try to be as true to ourselves as possible, and the other person is responsible for their part. Some people may not like it as you start to be responsible for your part and let go of the rest. They may not like it when you stop trying to take responsibility for what everyone else is feeling, when you realize you can't make anyone else happy. Only by being true to yourself do you have the ability to find contentment and, in turn, open up the possibility for others to find their own contentment. As you stop taking responsibility for others' happiness, and they stop taking responsibility for yours, you can finally have a true relationship, one based on love instead of fear.

I want to say again: being true to yourself is not the same thing as doing whatever feels good in the moment. It's not the same thing as running around like you are two years old saying, "I'm going to do whatever I want no matter who gets hurt or what the results are! It's all about me, me, me!" You are being true to yourself when you stop lying to yourself, when you stop selling yourself short, when you stop hurting yourself in order to please others. Because it will head you straight into your biggest fears, being true to yourself may actually take you down a harder path than the one of following along with everyone else. You may find yourself being judged and ridiculed by the people that you love and whose opinions you value.

Being true to your soul may lead you to making some very tough decisions. You may have to leave a relationship, change jobs, face difficult issues you have been trying to avoid. As you start to realize that you cause your spirit to contract when you lie, you start to understand that you must be true to yourself. If I lie, if I sell myself short, if I give in to the pressure of others, it might be easier right now in this moment, but I know it's hurtful to my heart and spirit.

So, doing what is true to yourself isn't always an easy route to take. You might be judged or ridiculed by those people in your life who base their idea of love on fear. You may lose some people who you thought really loved you unconditionally and who you felt were a vital part of your life. This can bring up a lot of hurt and loss but is often a necessary part of weeding the "false friends" from your life. As you open up space in your life, you will bring in people who will support you in your process and help nurture your true spirit. These people are your spiritual guides, ones who will help you see your beauty and gifts. They will provide true mirrors to you, based on love and acceptance, instead of the false mirrors provided by people who try to nurture your fears. As you bring into your life people whose healing journey is the same as yours, those people can provide true mirrors and bridges as you need them.

The people around you can be mirrors for you to see into yourself. If you see good qualities in the people around you, then those qualities are also in you. The more you spend time with people who have the qualities and traits to which you aspire, the more you can nurture and develop those qualities and traits in yourself. Similarly, the qualities you see and do not like in others are qualities also in you. If you spend time with people who have traits you do not like, you will tend to develop those traits too. For instance, if you spend time with people who are very negative or are judgmental, it can be very easy for you to become more negative and judgmental too. This is why it is important to choose carefully the people with whom you spend your time.

Spending time with people you admire will help you cultivate the qualities you like. Open up space and time in your life for people who will help nurture you on your journey. Let these people mirror back the qualities and traits you want to nurture and the ones you want to prune or change. They can help you to grow and expand, and then you can help them do the same thing. This is a relationship of being true witnesses to each other. When you are in a true witness relationship with someone, if that person triggers you, see what the trigger is revealing so that you can heal from it; encourage that person to do the same if triggered by you. It takes strong relationships to be able to love each other enough to delve into the issues that really trigger us.

My friends know I want them to tell their truth, even if I may not like hearing it. Sometimes I get triggered and need to take some time to reflect. Taking time to reflect is very important. You need to take the time to go beneath the triggers and the right or wrong of the situation to get to the deeper core issues that are really being triggered. When you are in a relationship with someone based in telling each other your truths, sometimes you will agree to disagree. Do you believe it is okay for someone to have a truth different from yours? Can you be okay with that? Can you give up the mentality that there is only *one* way? To help with your growth, surround yourself with people can help mirror your true self, people who help you uncover the real intentions behind your actions, people who love you enough that they also hold you accountable for your actions.

You will also have people in your life who will be bridges for you. These are the people who touch you so deeply that they help you see and feel your true beauty and brilliance. They act as a bridge—that is, they help you feel connected—to your truth and to divine love in a way you have not felt previously. It can be very easy to fall into wanting to make these people responsible for your feeling divine love and for the love itself that you feel. By making such people responsible in this way, you truly believe you will collapse without them in your life. You fall into believing that without them, you will lose the connection to divine truth and love. Operating from this fear—the fear of scarcity—can stop you from taking the next step. The truth is these people are often meant to be your bridge for only a short time. They are in your life to show you how it can be and to help you as you build your *own* bridge. We are not meant to have such people be our permanent bridge. This doesn't mean they have to leave your life; but, you do need to learn to make your own bridge.

We are supposed to learn that we can connect to divine love and to our truth on our own, independent of others. These "bridge" people reveal to you what is already in you, and they can help you in your process, but you must build your own bridge to divine love and to your truth. This process can be very difficult and painful, especially if you have been taught there will be one person in your life that will be able to make you happy. You may want someone who touches you deeply in this way to be your bridge always, but it isn't possible. Every time you try to have someone else be your permanent bridge, instead of building your own, the bridge will collapse. If you feel joy when you are with this other person, and sadness when you are not, then you have equated the feeling of joy with being with that person. While these "bridge" people can help reveal the joy inside of you, real healing comes when you can build your own bridge to joy. This way you have access to joy regardless of who is with you. The same is true with love. When you have forgotten how to access love, other people can help you feel the love that is actually always there.

You may go through several cycles of using someone who touches you deeply as a bridge and then having that bridge collapse before you will build your own bridge. How does the bridge collapse? Something happens that leads you to believe the person let you down or otherwise disappointed you; the person fails to meet your expectations in some way. When this happens, you might feel the pain from all the times you felt someone let you down or felt someone's actions showed that they didn't love you because they didn't act the way you thought they should.

When a bridge in your life collapses, you might find yourself thinking, "I knew I shouldn't have trusted that person. I knew I shouldn't have opened my heart that much. I knew I would get hurt." This is actually an opportunity for you to see statements like these as lies. The truth is love is always there and has always been there. We are the ones who built the walls and the moat that keep us separated from love. And we are the ones who have to build the bridge over the moat and tear down the walls so we can feel the love again. These "bridge" people give us an express route to the love, but it can only be temporary.

Building your own bridge and tearing down the walls does not mean you will always live in a state of unending happiness and joy. But, when you do have times of feeling alone or unhappy, you know you have a way to reconnect. You know you have the power to return to love and do not have to depend on others to get you there. This power stems from remembering the love, peace, and state of calm are within you at all times. When you build your own bridge and don't depend on someone else to help you connect to love, you can truly be open to enter a relationship based on unconditional love.

At the outset, it can be very difficult to let go of what others think or of how they react. The key is being open enough to see the gifts and pitfalls in both the "positive" and the "negative" reactions. People who are reacting in a way that you feel to be judgmental or critical may be angels sent to help you get to the real truth under your actions. The judgments and criticisms of others can sometimes help you break through, leading you to your truth and to the strength to do what you know is true even if others do not agree. Judgments and criticisms may also lead you to see that the truths behind your actions were actually based in fear, and this in turn may help you reconnect to your real truth.

Those who praise and agree with you can help you to believe in yourself more. However, these people can also be devils in disguise who are actually pointing you down a road that reinforces your ego and takes you further from your truth. Whether you are praised or criticized, you need to reflect and be open to see and feel your truth at the core. People can be mirrors and bridges and can help you know that you want your own bridge, but you have to do the physical, mental, and spiritual work yourself. As the Bible says, God helps those who help themselves. The people who act as mirrors and bridges can help show you how it can be, but you have to do the work to make your path back to your true self.

When you build your own bridge to your true self, the reaction of others becomes less and less important. You will *know* your truth, and you have a path to your truth that is independent of anyone else. You will know the truth of your beauty and your worth because you can connect to true love, a love based on the spiritual truth that everyone is beautiful and perfect. The externals will always change depending on where you live and what laws are enforced at that time. The reactions and judgments of others will also always change. Do not base your worth on what others tell you, as it will never last. This is why healing has to do with you. If you are trying to change because you think it will give you an outcome you want—a new house, a relationship, money in your bank account—your bridge will continue to collapse. You have to want to heal and change because you are truly ready to live. You have to want to do this for yourself because, when push comes to shove, all you have is yourself, and you are accountable for your soul and your spirit.

## Chapter 31

*Example through Action*

I love Gandhi's famous statement, "You must be the change you wish to see in the world." It's so true. If you want to bring peace into the world, bring peace into your life. If you want to have more love, be more loving. If you want to help others heal, heal yourself. It's not about anyone else or anything else. If you want to help improve this world and you want to help others heal, work on healing yourself. As you heal yourself, you will give others the opportunity to heal. By being true—living from your true self, speaking your truth, acting from a place of growth and healing, and coming from a place of personal responsibility—you will give others the opportunity to do the same. By taking care of yourself, you can show others the benefit of taking care of themselves.

Taking care of yourself is not selfish; it's selfless. You can't help anyone else if you are sick and exhausted. Earlier in this book, I used the example of Jesus taking time to reconnect so that He could minister to others. All of the spiritual masters exemplify this same behavior. It is very important to do things to keep your body and spirit healthy and to keep you connected to the divine and to truth. How you do this is your personal choice. Get into a practice that feels right for you, and let that practice evolve and be dynamic as you continue along your journey. Group meditation, travel, being alone in nature, taking classes—your practice could be any of these or anything else that calls to your spirit.

Take time to care for yourself and continue to heal. This will help you stay centered and grounded, which in turn will allow you to help others. Take time to be quiet and still. This will allow you to conquer the fears that control you, and it will lead to true freedom. As you face and feel through the fears and lies, you will reach the calm center. This is empowerment, being in the present moment and making choices with awareness, instead of reacting from your fears.

By living your truth, you will give others the opportunity to do the same. You will be a living example, which is much more powerful than words. People will learn what they see, not what they are told. Live your truth and give others the space to make their choices. If you try to change someone else by telling them what they are doing is wrong, you will set up a power struggle. If you're on the receiving end of that approach, it feels forceful and you will resist it. Helping someone grow can be a very delicate dance and you may both end up stepping on each other's toes along the way. You need to pay attention to your intentions and your reactions in the growth process. It's also important to let go of the idea that you need to show someone else that they are "wrong." If you can focus instead on your part in an interaction, you will actually give the other person a chance to step into growth on their own.

When I was traveling with a friend a few years ago, I had a great experience that showed me exactly what it meant to focus on my part of an interaction. This friend struggles with fears, negativity, and judgment. It seemed like everything we saw—a car, a house, a person, a store... *everything*—was judged in one way or another. "Can you believe the color of that house? Did you see the shoes that person was wearing? My goodness! Can you believe they would wear their hair that way?!" On and on it went. And, every time she made a judgment,

I could feel myself getting irritated because she was judging. So, I was judging my friend for judging others!

At first, I wanted to try to make her see she shouldn't judge others. I wanted to change her behavior because I didn't like it. I had the mentality that she was wrong. I found myself starting to defend the people she was judging. When I did this, it just made us both tense. It would shut her down, I would stop talking, and we were both grumbling in our heads. Sound familiar? I am sure you have been in a similar situation.

Then I decided to focus on and play with my reactions. I started to observe my reactions and what it did to me. Instead of focusing on the fact that she should change, I started to see how I could grow. When she judged someone, I let myself feel what it brought up in me. I let myself feel what it would feel like if I believed the judgment she had made. How did I feel if I agreed with her and believed that the house was the wrong color? I noticed when I believed a judgment that wasn't true to me, it made my diaphragm tighten up and I would feel the tension spread through my body. After I felt that, I would see what it felt like if I let go of my judgment and opened myself to whatever had been judged. I opened to the idea that the color of the house was perfect just how it was because the person who owned the house liked it. I found that when I let go of the judgment, my diaphragm opened and I felt an ease spread throughout my body. I now had awareness of what judging did to my body and had a choice to make. I could choose to judge and tighten down or to let go of judgment and feel open and expansive.

Some judgments were easy to let go as I didn't have anything invested in what was being judged; I didn't have a strong belief either way. I really didn't care what style of shoes the person wore, as I usually choose my shoes based on comfort and not on style. If I did have a stronger belief on a subject, then I found that it was harder for me to let it go. For instance, I was raised to believe that guys should not have long hair, so it took me a little longer to let go of that idea. Beliefs that are emotionally charged or that are pushed upon us hard when we are growing up can be harder to let go. I just let myself play with it and gave myself time while

I continued to be aware of the tension in my body. When you become aware of the physical consequences that come from judging, it helps to see why you should learn to let go of judgments.

My next step was to see if I could respond to my friend's judging something by actually saying out loud, "They must like it that way." When I did so, I kept connected with my body, as I now could use it as a lie detector. If I still had judgment against my friend or against what she was judging, then my diaphragm would tighten. That would indicate to me I still had things to let go. If I could say it without any judgment and without trying to change her, then my body would stay open and at ease. I continued to play with this throughout the entire trip. I was using this only as a way to help myself grow and had let go of trying to get her to change or grow. I had let go of any expectations on her part. I focused on my judgments and my reactions. I kept feeling what it was like to judge my friend, or to judge the situation, and what it felt like if I opened and let go.

It was neat to see how focusing on my thoughts and judgments even more than normal helped to keep me open and relaxed. Usually, my judgments would stay in my head, and I didn't bring my full attention to them. My friend's judging allowed me to see how many judgments were passing through my mind all the time. By responding out loud—"They must like it that way." or something similar—I had the opportunity to feel whether I had truly let the judgment go or was just fooling myself. It became easier and easier to remain calm and relaxed with this person while she judged others.

My big surprise and "Ah-ha" moment came toward the end of the trip. As we were heading to the airport, my friend looked at a house and said, "Oh my gosh! Can you believe they painted their house that color?" and, before I could say anything, she took a breath and said, "Oh, but they must like it that way." And I could tell she had been able to let go of the judgment and really felt that way. I almost fell out of my chair! It was such a beautiful example to me of the statement "You must be the change you wish to see in the world." I helped my friend have options on how to deal with her judgment and negativity by helping myself come to terms with it. I showed her an example of how she could be if she let it go. This happened because I wasn't trying to tell her how to do it, I just did it. She could see and feel the change in me, and that was more powerful than any words could have been. By going into my triggers and coming to peace within myself, I allowed her the space to do the same. That gave her the opportunity to make her own choice, to build her own bridge.

It can be difficult to do this. We can get caught up in trying to make someone understand. Sometimes people do need to be nudged along in their journey, but I have found more and more that example is the best teacher. By not trying to change others and instead just being true to yourself and progressing with your healing, by looking at how something triggers you and growing, you will give others the opportunity to change and heal. One of the best examples you can live is being gentle with yourself. Don't hold yourself up to perfection; doing so will just reinforce your ability to judge yourself and won't lead anyone to healing or growth. We're all doing the best we know how to do at any time in our life, and it takes time and persistence for growth to occur. Be gentle with yourself when you slip back into old habits, and be gentle with others as they do too.

It's going to take some thought and some time, but as you are gentle with yourself and learn how to love and forgive yourself, and then act accordingly, you give others the best thing you could give: the opportunity to do the same themselves. People really do learn what they see and not what they hear. It doesn't matter how much you tell people how they should be, but showing them through genuine actions not only helps you to heal but also helps the whole world to heal.

Section 6

*Putting It All Together*

# Chapter 32

## *Use All You have Learned*

In the beginning of this book, I said your path would be different from anyone else's, and I want to remind you of that again here. Take what you need from this book and from other resources—other books, lectures, classes, interactions with other students and masters, your own life experiences—and uncover *your* truth. Each resource that you examine will make suggestions. Some will propose or stipulate rules, principles, and protocols. In every case, it will be up to you to determine whether some particular aspect of what a given resource offers is right for you at the moment.

You may find yourself connecting to some resources now that don't work for you later on and vice versa. Always remember the process is dynamic, and even your truths may change over time. Avoid the trap of believing your opinions and beliefs should never change. Always be open to look at and hear things with a fresh and open mind, even if you feel you have heard them a million times. There is always more to learn. The only way for you to know your truth is by the way it feels to your body and spirit. Every thought, every intention, every act will either enhance your spirit and help your soul expand or cause your spirit to contract. Only by clearing your triggers and your fears, and feeling what helps your soul grow and expand, will you know what works for you.

You're going to need to go in and uncover your truths by systematically evaluating every one of your beliefs, thoughts, and judgments. Remember to include feeling as a guide in finding your truth. You will not get to your truth by thinking; you will know your truth through the felt sense. In evaluating your beliefs, thoughts, and judgments, you're seeking to find out which ones are true to you and which you just accept because you were told to believe them. As you go inward to uncover and heal, you will be able to expand outwards and connect at a much deeper level to everyone.

As you heal yourself and bring more love to yourself, you will be able to accept and love others more easily, without conditions or expectations. This process is not about becoming self-centered; it's about really connecting with everyone else through love. It is about developing a strong sense of your true self. As you take the time to feel and heal your hurts and clear your lies, you will be able to connect to others in a compassionate and loving way. So, as you heal yourself, you truly do expand out to help others heal.

Add the universal principles I discussed in section 3 to any of your self-healing practices. Apply the universal principles to your work with positive intentions, co-creation ideas, affirmations, meditation, yoga, body techniques, and self-treatment. And of course, add the felt sense to everything you do. Regardless of what you're doing, feel your body and ask, "Is this helping my body to open or is it causing my body to tighten down?" Take your time; it takes time for change to occur. Meet each situation at its barrier; if you use force you will get resistance. Everything's connected; by healing yourself, you help the entire universe heal. You have to feel your truths. Truth is detected from your felt sense, not from your head. The feeling component is one of the most important and often overlooked aspects of healing. When you set your goals, when you state what you want, feel into your body and notice how it responds to the goals and statements. When you get triggered, feel. Add the feeling component to every aspect of your growth process so you can be guided to your truths and uncover the fears and the lies.

When you are trying to determine whether you have healed fully or still have layers to work through, connect into your body to make the determination. You will know you have completely healed everything you need to heal around an issue when you can talk about the issue and you feel your body is completely open and at ease. If you still have parts to clear and heal, you will feel a reaction in your body. It might be tension, bracing, pain, or any other sensation. Your body is like a tuning fork; if you are talking about an issue and there are still elements of that issue that need to heal, an area of your body will be triggered just like a tuning fork being struck. You will feel a vibration in your body; you will have a sensation triggered.

The only way to tell whether you've healed an issue fully is to take your words and feel them into your body. You can convince yourself you have healed if you keep it in the level of your head. You need to feel the reactions in your body to discover the truth. When you drop the words into your body, if you feel it tensing or you feel pain or other sensations anywhere in it, it's telling you there are still places that aren't healed. You may be able to connect with the triggered area, and get it to open and release, just by being aware and by feeling what comes up. Take time to feel, breathe into the area, and give your body permission to open and soften. Remind your body and yourself that you are safe and give yourself permission to feel whatever you need. If your body doesn't open, it may need some self-treatment or bodywork in that area to help it open up so that you can feel fully and release whatever needs to be healed. If you attempt to heal only by staying in your head and trying to change your thoughts, you will produce only temporary change and find yourself continually fighting the programming and your tissue memory.

As you learn how to feel your truths, you will become truly empowered. The healing and growth journey is not about having someone else tell you how you should feel or what you should do; it's about becoming the master of your true self. As you read books and listen to teachers, be open to asking yourself, "Does this technique, this book, this person empower me or is it about taking away my power?" Don't give away your power anymore. If someone tells you they can heal or fix you, they are taking away your power. Seek out and find the people who want to help you learn how to heal yourself. These are the people who will guide you to true growth and empowerment. This doesn't mean you should avoid people who will challenge you. You need to find someone who is strong enough in their true self to be an honest guide for you, someone who will hold the light up to help you see places you can't, or perhaps don't want to, see.

Start asking yourself in every situation of your life, "Does this empower me, is this leading me to become more true to myself, or am I giving away my power and limiting my growth in this situation?" Ask yourself the following questions, and really take the time to explore the answers with compassionate honesty.

- How am I giving my power away?

- How am I selling myself?

- In what ways am I bartering my spirit and soul because I'm afraid?

- What advice am I being given that I am not following because I am afraid of the changes that would happen?

Another important point to remember is that this is a dynamic process that will continue to evolve *for the rest of your life. There is no finish line.* So many people get frustrated and stop their journey because they believe that false and damaging lie. They believe if you do it "right," you will reach a point in your spiritual growth after which you will no longer have any chaos or challenges in your life. This is not a truth. There's not an end point to your process. As long as you're on this earth, you're going to be working on connecting the spiritual with the physical and working with beliefs and thoughts.

Some people believe the growth process continues through multiple lifetimes, while others believe we have only one life on earth. It doesn't matter if you believe in a single life or in multiple lifetimes. What does matter is that you know as long as you're here you're going to continue to have opportunities to heal and grow, to expand and increase your connection to everyone and everything. Some people believe that if they reach a certain place in their journey, they will obtain everlasting happiness. This is true if you consider happiness to be the ability to accept everything that happens without judgment, to make a total surrender into what is. But, if you believe happiness depends on you receiving everything you desire and on every situation working out as you wish, you will actually move into a place of suffering. Happiness occurs when you stop trying to obtain or create things that will make you happy. Happiness can be in every moment of your experience as soon as you let go of the belief that any moment should be any different from how it is. Feeling this form of happiness is absolute contentment that stems from an absolute and unwavering belief that everything happens for a reason.

The following is a list of general stages you may find yourself going through on your healing journey. The stages start at the state where you are completely disconnected from your truths and from the divine and progress to the state where you feel complete connection. This is not a protocol; it is a list of some of the potential points along your journey. Sometimes you will find yourself starting at stage 1 and moving through stage by stage to stage 12. Sometimes you will skip stages. Sometimes you will be at a later stage and then something comes up that takes you back to a much earlier stage because there is something at that earlier stage that needs to be felt; then you may jump all the way to the last stage. This is a dynamic process, and it will not be linear. This list is just a way to give you some idea of some of the potential stages. You may find it fun or useful to keep a journal of the stages in which you find yourself. Keeping such a journal can help you see what is changing as you progress along.

## Stages of Growth

1. **Unable to connect**—You are unable to connect to your truth
   or to the divine. You can't see anything in your current trigger
   that will lead to growth. The idea of growth or self-discovery
   doesn't even resonate with you at this point.

2. **React and pull out**—You are triggered and you shut down.
   You may leave the situation physically or emotionally. You stop
   feeling. There is no potential for growth. This can trap you into
   being numb.

3. **React with judgments**—You fight the trigger and the situation.
   You believe it shouldn't have happened and it is not your fault.
   You blame everyone else for your problems. You are starting to
   feel the uncomfortable feelings, but you project what you are
   feeling onto others or onto the external situation. It can be very
   easy to get stuck in this stage, as it can feel good to blame others.
   There is a rush with the drama, and it can be easy to fall into a
   "me vs. them" mentality. It can lead to wanting battles so you
   can "win" and be "right."

4. **Feel with judgments**—You are able to stay with the feelings
   more and you start to open yourself up to the possibility of
   looking at the situation as growth, but you are still not able to
   let go of the judgments.

5. **Soften with judgment**—You are now starting to surrender and
   open up to growth. You start to feel through the sensations
   you were trying to avoid. You may start turning the judgments
   against yourself instead of judging everyone else. You need to
   foster compassionate awareness, or you may get stuck in the
   victim mentality of blaming yourself. You also need to start to
   develop self-love.

6. **Soften without judgment**—You start to progress into surrender,
   acceptance, and forgiveness. Believing forgiveness is about

right and wrong can be a stumbling block here. Remember forgiveness is about becoming empowered.

7.  **Being able to witness**—You can step outside the situation and change your perspective. You can see the situation from another person's perspective and you can also put someone else in your situation. Both of these will help you let go of some of the beliefs preventing you from forgiving yourself and others. You can start to be open to the belief that everything happens for a reason.

8.  **Becoming aware**—You are now becoming aware of how your beliefs and judgments affect you. You can feel in your body and feel how it would feel to hang on or to let go. You are aware now of how your beliefs and judgments are either enhancing or contracting your spirit. You are better able to distinguish the voice of your truth from the voices of fear.

9.  **Making a choice**—You now understand the consequences of your choices. You have stepped into the responsibility stage. You know you are responsible for your own reactions. You know fully you have the power to act in a way that can enhance, expand, or contract your spirit. This is a time when it's important to remind yourself change can take time. When you find yourself making choices that contract your spirit, you will need to be as gentle and forgiving with yourself as you would with those you love. Even though you know you want to make choices to expand your spirit, those choices may be very scary. This is a stage where people will start to notice you changing.

10. **Empowering**—It now becomes easier and easier to make the choices that will expand your spirit and that are true to you. You have reached the point where the opinions of others do not matter to you as much as does being true to yourself. This is a phase where you are able to connect to the divine more easily and to hear your true guidance.

11. **Acceptance and forgiveness**—You believe truly everything happens for a reason. You are able to let go of the judgment of the situation, and you can open up to the gifts and the growth. You are not only able to forgive yourself and everyone involved, but you also are able to see there was nothing to forgive in the first place. You can start to feel what divine love (unconditional love) is about.

12. **Healing**—You are completely connected to the divine and to the truths of unconditional love and acceptance. The situation has been fully healed. You can see and accept the gifts. You can feel the connection between you, the divine, and everyone else. This is a stage of complete love where you see and know that if you love yourself, you love everyone. You know that if you think or act in a harmful way toward yourself, you are harming everyone, and conversely, if you think or act in a harmful way toward anyone else, you are harming yourself. In this stage you are no longer separate from the divine or anything else.

## Balance

Healing and growing are a balance of expanding out and going inward. Some people believe that growth occurs only by peeling away the layers, that you have to go deeper into yourself to grow. Others argue growth can occur only by going outside of yourself and connecting to the whole. I want to remind you again to watch out for the "only one way" philosophy in the context of growth. Growth is always about all directions. The growth process will be about both going outward to expand and going inward to uncover. Both will lead you to deeper awareness of yourself and also to a deeper connection with everyone else and the divine. Going in all directions, the possibilities are infinite. You can always go in further and you can always expand out further.

As an example, let's take a judgment and see how both paths can lead to healing. Consider the lie that we should fear people of a race different from our own. This belief is used to keep you separate from others, which makes you different from others; this fear can be used to manipulate you. To start the growth process, you can take the time to go internally and uncover where you first started to take on this belief; this can lead to growth. Or, you could look at expanding outward to establish a connection between you and people of this different race. Both paths will lead you to uncover fears, lies, and truths. As you connect with a trigger, you can feel it through to uncover your truths. As you establish your truth, you can expand that truth out to apply not only to this trigger but to all similar triggers.

As you challenge what you were told is truth, uncovering both the lies and the real truth, you can be open to feel and see the connection between everyone. This will help you expand well beyond your little world or community, and see and connect with the entire world. As you go in and uncover and heal the false beliefs that you hold and that lead you to judge yourself, you will be able to let go of your judgments of others. This pattern of in and out is very similar to the pattern of breathing. Bringing in and then releasing out. Opening and expanding.

There will always be more gifts to discover and more layers you can heal. Both paths—going deeper within and expanding out—will lead to a deeper connection to yourself and all living beings. As with every aspect of growth, the skill is finding a dynamic balance between the two sides. You need to go in and uncover your true self to detach the tethers that keep causing you to *re*act, instead of to act, in the moment. This will free you up to feel the connection to every living thing in this world. As you establish this balance, all of your relationships will become deeper. The shifting back and forth is a cycle; you find your balance point in each moment, knowing the balance point will change too. You may find you are more comfortable going one way rather than the other; this indicates the way on which you need to focus: the one that is uncomfortable. To grow, you need to be comfortable being uncomfortable. Do the things that challenge you physically, emotionally, and spiritually, and, as you do so, you will conquer your fears and become truly empowered and free.

Chapter 33

*Limitless*

We are all limitless, and we are all as expansive as this universe. Remember you are a part of the divine, and you are always loved and accepted unconditionally. Also remember to love yourself and to be easy on yourself. Each one of us here on earth is just fumbling through the best we know how. It is truly a dance of life; sometimes you'll step on other people's toes, and sometimes they'll step on yours. Sometimes you will need to lead and other times to follow. Sometimes you will find yourself fighting for control. Sometimes you will feel yourself moving with ease and grace, and other times you will fall flat on your face. The key is to get back up and dance again. This is your life. Don't sit on the sidelines and watch people dance. Join in! Take risks! Live! Continue to see yourself in each person you meet, and remember to appreciate the small things in life.

Set your goals as big as you want, but just remember to focus on the process, not the outcome. As you grow, you will reach a point where the material means less and less and the spiritual means more and more.

True growth can start to occur when you lose the fear of the physical world and start to live more from your spiritual truths.

Focus on changing 1%. Focus on your current step instead of always looking at the peak. As you take the pressure off yourself, the dynamic leaps can occur. If you always focus on the end point and the fact that you are not there yet, it's just going to slow you down. Be easy on yourself and consider 1% a huge change. Remember you are already the person you want to be. You already are the brilliant masterpiece. Your job is to just uncover the parts that are hiding your beauty.

You are more powerful than you ever imagined. Transition and growth can be easier than you thought. If you want it to be hard, it will be. If you are open for it to be easy, it will be as easy as it can be. You will have struggles and hard times, but suffering comes from resisting what is, from resisting the process that must occur.

We all have hidden rooms filled with treasures and talents and gifts. We will continue to discover these throughout our entire life. This isn't about discovering the things about us that we don't like; it's about clearing those things so we can let our gifts and our talents shine.

Remember to spend as much time cultivating what you want to grow as you do weeding out the things you do not like or that you want to change. Anything to which you give your attention and focus will grow. Fertilize and put water on the plants, trees, and flowers that you want to grow. Do the same with your thoughts and beliefs. Cultivate the thoughts, beliefs, and actions that will head you in the direction you want to go. As negative thoughts and actions come up, be aware of them without encouraging them. If those negative thoughts and actions keep happening, then it's time to feel your way through to the core of the issue.

Life is constantly in motion. Life is not stable; it is dynamic, always changing. Your growth process will be the same. Some days you'll be able to see and feel the beauty within every cell of your body. You'll see the brilliance in the sunset and feel the same brilliance within you.

There will be times when you feel the divine, feel unconditional love to the core of your body. You will feel alive and feel connected to every living organism on this planet. Some days you'll feel like the sun has set forever. You will not be able to connect to anything, and you will feel like God has deserted you. This is why it is important to remember the spiritual law "This too shall pass." When you're in moments of joy, bliss, and peace, enjoy them because they will pass. When you feel desolate and like you can't go on, hang on because this too will pass.

Above all, remember you already are that which you seek. So, what are you waiting on? What are you afraid of? You are already what you want to be, so there is no possible way to fail! It's time to live, and it's time to reclaim your brilliance. Your path will take you to enrichment beyond any you could have ever imagined. Notice the word *enrichment*. Enrichment has nothing to do with houses and cars; enrichment of the soul cannot be purchased.

All it takes is a step, so start right now. Step away and start your journey. And, when you hit a crossroads or when you doubt, start to feel your way through to healing.

# *Book List*

In this book, I have mentioned several authors and books that have helped me on my journey. Here is a list of some of those books, arranged alphabetically by author. You may find some of these particular books helpful, or you may be drawn to other books by these authors. You might also find, as you look for these books online or in bookstores, you are drawn to other the works of other authors. This list contains just a few of the books I have read along the way. There is an endless supply of information that can help you along your journey; when you need some, it will come along.

John F. Barnes: *Healing Ancient Wounds: The Renegade's Wisdom*

Pema Chödrön: *Start Where You Are*; *The Places that Scare You*

Paulo Coelho: *The Alchemist*; *Brida*; *The Witch of Portobello*; *Adelph*

Deepak Chopra: *How to Know God*

Lee Coit: *Listening*; *Being*

Wayne Dyer: *The Ten Secrets to Success*; *Choosing Your Own Greatness*

Linda Kohanov: *The Tao of Equus*; *Riding Between the Worlds*

Caroline Myss: *Spiritual Madness*; *Invisible Acts of Power*; *Defy Gravity*; *Why People Don't Heal*; *Your Power to Create*; *Anatomy of the Spirit*

Mark Nepo: *The Book of Awakening*

Don Miguel Ruiz: *The Four Agreements*; *Mastery of Love*; *Voice of Knowledge*

Colin Tipping: *Radical Forgiveness*

Eckhart Tolle: *The Power of Now*; *A New Earth*

CATHY COVELL is the owner of Motion for Life Treatment Center in Orland, Indiana. This is a treatment center that focuses on helping people and animals on their healing journeys.

Cathy is a Physical Therapist and Massage Therapist who specializes in Myofascial Release. Cathy treats humans and also animals with this technique along with a dynamic integrated program depending on what each participant needs. The clinic helps rehabilitate humans from pain and injuries along with helping abused and injured animals.

Cathy also teaches seminars instructing people how to treat horses using Myofascial Release and has other seminars to help with improving awareness and progressing along the healing path.

For more information, go to the website: www.motionforlife.net.